Post Oil America and a renewable energy policy leads to the abrogation of the Middle East to China.

CONTENTS

Abstract

This paper examines the effects of a renewable energy policy on American foreign policy. As the US weans itself from oil it will accelerate the already occurring geopolitical shift in the Middle East from a region dominated by the United States to one that will be dominated by China. As a result of this shift, the US will lose access and influence in the region and realignments will occur among nation states leading the Saudis to grow their military and accelerate their quest for nuclear weapons. Unencumbered by the US, Saudi Arabian domestic policies will shift towards the more extreme versions of Wahhabism, leading towards an even harder stance towards Israel.

In attempt to examine the effects, the paper will detail the importance of oil to the United States (and world). The paper will provide historical detail on why oil is integral to US national strategy and the various means that policy makers and Presidents have used oil to advance American interests. That will be coupled with Saudi Arabian and Chinese interests in the region and how an American renewable energy policy will only hasten the effects of the eventual turnover of American control of the Persian Gulf to the Chinese.

"The oil can is mightier than the sword."

-Senator Everett Dirksen

Introduction:

Pick up a paper or watch the news today and one hears or reads the argument that it is critical that the US be weaned off of oil for a variety of reasons, including concerns over "peak oil", global warming and climate change, and national security. One of the more shrill cries, especially after 9/11, is the need to reduce the US consumption of oil as it is critical to our national security. Most of the cries end there without any real explanation as to the urgency. Those that do provide any analysis on this issue generally state the same three issues. First is the fear that a terrorist incident on an oil rig or large refinery could disrupt the oil supply. The second is the concern that one of the many straits around the world could be blockaded to disrupt the flow of oil around the world. The last is the case that the US is paying millions of dollars to those oil-exporting countries whose interests in the world conflict with ours. Frankly, there is logic missing in all three concerns listed above.

First, whatever energy source is chosen will always be vulnerable to attack. Terrorists can just as easily destroy nuclear plants, wind farms, hydroelectric dams, and large solar arrays. Second, the economic vitality of the global community depends on the major shipping straits in the world. A rogue state may well blockade a strait, but many straits can be circumnavigated and it is highly unlikely the world community would idly standby and allow a blockade to happen. The last issue ignores the fact that US purchasing power does have influence over the oil exporting countries of the world and it is not necessarily true that the world would be better off if the US had no influence in these oil-exporting countries. And further, it completely forgets that all of the world's oil is traded using the US dollar and that much of the money that pays for the oil from oil-exporting nations ends up buying large volumes of American debt. Unfortunately, no one has truly explored the second and third order effects on US foreign policy in a post-oil America. What would the geopolitical implications be of a US that doesn't need oil?

As Daniel Yergin writes in his Pulitzer Prize winning book *The Prize, The Epic Quest for Oil, Money, and Power,* "three great themes underlie oil…the first is the rise and development of capitalism and modern business…the second is that of oil as a commodity intimately intertwined with national strategies and global politics and power and the third is how ours has become a Hydrocarbon Society and we, in the language of anthropologists, Hydrocarbon Man."[1] Oil is the lifeblood of the American economy and by extension, the American way of life. This single commodity has been the concern of every element of national power applied by Presidents, policy makers, and strategists for more than the last half century.

There are many reports advocating policies to reduce our dependence on foreign oil for the reasons listed above, but there is so far no evidence of a strategy to do so successfully. The larger question of a policy to reduce our dependence on foreign oil is the geopolitical and strategic impact. "For the nearly five decades of the Cold War, US Middle Eastern policy was defined by the geostrategic threat from the Soviet Union and the need to protect oil interests. US policy also hinged on managing the Arab-Israeli conflict and, in recent decades, containing radical Islamist forces."[2]

Let there be no doubt that oil is a vital interest to the United States. Oil is a ubiquitous product in the US economy fueling the vast majority of the transportation system and providing a

---

[1] Daniel Yergin, *The Prize, The Epic Quest for Oil, Money, and Power* (New York: Touchstone, 1991), 14-15.

[2] "Part 5: The Obama Administration and the Middle East," Stratfor, Global Intelligence, http://www.stratfor.com/analysis/20090218_part_4_obama_administration_and_middle_east (accessed February 23, 2009).

vital ingredient to hundreds of products. In 2006, the buying and selling of oil globally accounted for a $1.7 trillion dollar business. One third of that market is the US share that exceeds $500 billion dollars. As a comparison, $500 billion in US oil purchases in 2006 would rank oil purchases by the US 27th on a world GDP list.[3] That is an enormous amount of market power that the US wields.

Oil's impact on the US economy is the reason it is a vital interest. Cheap oil equals prosperity for the American people and prosperity equals the fulfillment of the grand strategy of America for Presidents and policy makers. As such, ensuring the free flow of oil and access to oil has been a means for successive Presidents to project our freedom and ideals around the world. As the fuel that drives the largest economy in the world, oil becomes leverage in the high stakes game of geopolitics. Oil is a tool for Presidents and policy makers that can be utilized to exercise national power from economic trade deals because of the enormous market power the US wields, to diplomatic alliances and agreements, to the exercise of military power. "We talk about hard power and soft power, but the twenty-first century could also be the century of oil power, exercised not only by the producing nations, but also by smart consuming nations."[4] The authors are half right in their statement. Oil does equate to power but contrary to their statement, oil power has already been used extensively, by both producers and consumers, in the exercise of national power. US concern over oil played a central role in numerous policy decisions in the last 60 years. In fact, oil is the central reason why the US is involved so extensively in the Middle East.

---

[3] Detailed footnotes for these figures are spelled out in Chapter 3.

[4] Steve Yetiv and Lowell Feld, "*America's Oil Market Power,*" World Policy Institute, 2008, 53.

In the quest to reduce the consumption of oil, the US is failing to see the larger impact of a renewable energy policy. Reverse engineering over 60 years of policy, strategy, diplomacy, and military efforts to ensure the free flow and access to oil will inevitably cause a "vacuum" of American access, presence, and influence in a highly volatile region; raise the specter of larger militaries; cause an increasing need for nuclear weapons; shift security and cooperation guarantees; and disrupt the US economy and foreign policy. The implementation of a renewable energy policy begins to shift US prominence in the Persian Gulf to one dominated by China, resulting in US loss of strategic access and influence in an already volatile region. China presently practices a pure form of realpolitik in the region as they do not demand much of their energy suppliers nor care about the attendant politics of the region so long as they have a reliable oil stream. Saudi Arabia, as the largest producer of oil and keeper of the Islamic faith, will look to maintain their hold on power and will recognize the shift from the US to China and with it their security umbrella that has been provided by the US. Saudi Arabia will be happy to increase their relationship with China as that not only brings them large revenues for their national budget, it also brings a "no questions asked" policy of arms purchases and a lack of concern over Saudi's domestic policies, their quest for nuclear weapons, or their stance towards Israel. As the US weans itself from oil it will accelerate the already occurring geopolitical shift in the Middle East from a region dominated by the United States to one that will be dominated by China. As a result of this shift, the US will lose access and influence in the region and realignments will occur among nation states leading the Saudis to grow their military and accelerate their quest for nuclear weapons. Unencumbered by the US, Saudi Arabian domestic policies will shift towards the more extreme versions of Wahhabism, leading towards an even harder stance towards Israel.

Optimism to reduce US consumption of foreign oil without a well thought out strategy is fraught with risk. "Optimism and pessimism can be perilous as attitudes that undergird policy. But of the two, optimism is apt to kill with greater certainty. Whereas pessimism may inspire a grand strategy, and especially defense preparation, that triggers responsive countermoves abroad, optimism has the potential to risk national safety and even international order more generally."[5]

For purposes of scope, the paper will focus on the United States, Saudi Arabia and China. The paper will flow from the beginning with a chapter detailing why oil is important to the US and how it fits into the American Grand Strategy. The next chapter will detail what oil means to the economy. Chapter three will spell out in great detail the various ways oil has caused US Presidents to form policies across economic, diplomatic, and military lines of power to ensure the free flow of and access to oil for the United States. Chapter four will detail the feasibility, acceptability, and suitability of a renewable energy policy. Chapter five will bring in China and cover their rise to prominence in recent years and with it an expanding presence in the Middle East. Although Saudi Arabia will be covered in some detail through the paper, Chapter six will concentrate on Saudi Arabia to ensure that its concerns and national interests are covered. Chapter seven will detail the confluence of events and what they will mean for a declining US presence and influence, a rising China, and Saudi's position in the middle and then the paper will conclude with the implications of the events.

---

[5] Colin Gray, *Another Blood Century* (London: Phoenix, 2004), 34.

"The reason the US has a legitimate and critical interest in seeing the Persian Gulf oil continue to flow . . . is simply that the global economy built over the last 50 years rests on a foundation of inexpensive, plentiful oil"

-Kenneth Pollack

Chapter 1: Oil is a Vital Interest

Kenneth Pollack goes on to say in the quote above that "if that foundation were removed the global economy would collapse."[6] It is safe to say that Mr. Pollack is not overstating the case. As this paper will detail in the following pages of this chapter, oil is quite literally the energy, power and lubrication that runs the US economy. It is the lifeblood of the economic engine of America. That engine leads to prosperity, and prosperity for Americans is a function of grand strategy therefore making oil a vital interest.

Oil is considered "the world's most valuable resource" and has become ubiquitous to American life since our emergence from the Civil War and the beginning of the industrial age.[7] "Of the many new industries that emerged after the Civil War, none was more important than oil refining."[8] Much of the history of America is based on the confluence at the turn of the 19th century of the internal combustion engine, the model T car, the airplane and oil. In just over 100 years, the US has gone from horse and buggy transportation that traveled five or six miles a day to modes and means of transportation that have taken us to the moon in the span of hours. The invention of the car and airplane gave us the ability to ship goods and services to more locations in a faster amount of time. Further exploitation of oil and its properties led us to extract various fuels and chemicals that have such wide ranging applications as fertilizers for farming and the chemical basis for plastics and synthetics.

---

[6] Kenneth Pollack, "Securing the Gulf," *Foreign Affairs* 82, no. 4 (Jul/Aug 2003): 2.

[7] Ian Rutledge, *Addicted to Oil: America's Relentless Drive for Energy Security* (London: I.B. Tauris, 2005), 1.

[8] Robert Heilbroner and Aaron Singer, *The Economic Transformation of America: 1600 to the Present,* (San Diego: Harcourt Brace Jovanovich, 1984), 177.

Oil and the combustion engine not only changed American business and American life, but oil also brought about the age of mechanized warfare. "In the twentieth century, people had to learn how to run a war economy and the armed forces on oil rather than coal and horsepower."[9] The fuel that has kept the lamp of America burning for millions of Americans and citizens of the world for over 100 years has been oil. It is the backbone of our economy and as such is absolutely vital.

According to statistics from the Energy Information Administration's website, "the U.S. produces 10% of all the [world's] oil yet consumes 24%."[10] As another example, the US consumption of oil has risen from approximately 5 million barrels a day in late 1940s to over 20 million barrels a day in 2007.[11]

There are many reasons why oil is of vital national interest to the US and other industrialized countries around the world. First, oil is not a fungible commodity as it is not easily replaced or substituted by another commodity. Second, it accounts for over 95% of transportation costs and is a key ingredient in over 140 different products.[12] Oil is refined into gasoline, kerosene, jet fuel, heating oil, plastics, synthetic rubber, fertilizers, herbicides, and even heart valves, to name just a few. Further, this is a country that is run by machines which are fueled by oil. Interrupt the supply of oil and you not only stop the transportation of goods across America and the world but you also affect the ability of the vast majority of Americans to get to work. Americans intuitively understand the impact of having no oil. Oil has transformed the

---

[9] Gray, 49.

[10] "'How Dependent Are We on Foreign Oil?'," Energy Information Administration, http://tonto.eia.doe.gov/energy_in_brief/foreign_oil_dependence.cfm (accessed November 15, 2008).

[11] "Annual Energy Review," Energy Information Administration, http://www.eia.doe.gov/emeu/aer/pdf/pages/sec5.pdf, (accessed December 3, 2008).

[12] "There's a Lot of Life in a Barrel of Oil," American Petroleum Institute, http://www.api.org/classroom/tools/upload/oilfacts_rgb.pdf (accessed November 12, 2008).

way we do business and created whole new businesses. Oil has led the way to suburban living and a reshaping of the way Americans live. Oil has even changed our culture and the way Americans live.

Presidents, strategists, and policy makers have understood over the last 60 years the importance of oil to the grand strategy for a prosperous America. The need for oil is a need to fuel the economy of America. And the need to fuel the economy of America is part and parcel of the grand strategy of America. In the preamble to the US Constitution it states:

> We the People of the United States, in Order to form a more perfect Union, establish Justice, insure domestic Tranquility, provide for the common defence, promote the general Welfare, and secure the Blessings of Liberty to ourselves and our Posterity, do ordain and establish this Constitution for the United States of America.[13]

In order to "provide for the common defence, and promote the general Welfare" of the United States a strong economy is needed and oil empowers that economy. To paraphrase President Calvin Coolidge, the business of America is business.[14] Prosperity for Americans has been an enduring goal passed down to us from our Founding Fathers. Presidents and policy makers have a history on ensuring the free flow of and the strategic access to oil. President George H.W. Bush writes in his National Security Strategy that "A healthy and growing economy to ensure opportunity for individual prosperity and resources for national endeavors at home and abroad."[15] President Clinton's National Security Strategy quotes the preamble to the Constitution and then states ". . . interests are ultimately defined by our security requirements.

---

[13] U. S. Constitution, Preamble.

[14] President Calvin Coolidge speech, "The Press Under a Free Government," given to the American Society of Newspaper Editors in Washington, D.C. on January 17, 1925.

[15] President George H.W. Bush, *National Security Strategy of the United States,* http://www.fas.org/man/docs/918015-nss.htm, accessed January 23, 2009.

Such requirements start with our physical defense and economic well being."[16] Presidents have applied all elements of national power in achieving this goal.[17] Oil has been a means to achieve this end and everything in the arsenal of national power has been used, from alliances and alignments, to trade deals, business deals, economic sanctions, and of course, war.

Oil is considered a vital interest because it underpins so much of the US economy, which is central to the prosperity and defense of America. The next chapter will explain in greater detail just how important oil is to the US economy.

---

[16] President William Jefferson Clinton, *National Security Strategy of Engagement and Enlargement,* http://www.fas.org/spp/military/docops/national/1996stra.htm, accessed January 23, 2009.

[17] For the purposes of this paper National Power equates to any Diplomatic, Economic, or Military means to achieve their goals.

"To keep a lamp burning we have to keep putting oil into it"

-Mother Teresea

Chapter 2: Oil and the Economy

The magnitude of oil's impact on the American economy and the formation of our foreign policy are hard to overstate. In terms of sheer monetary cost it is hard to think of any other substance that commands so much money. As an example, according to the figures from the US Energy Information Website, world crude oil production in 2006 amounted to 73.54 million barrels a day (including lease condensate, but excluding natural gas plant liquids).[18] Multiply that amount by the average price of crude in 2006 of $66.43[19] per barrel and the oil trade is worth $4.8 billion dollars daily. Extrapolate this sum to a yearly total and one finds that the oil trade is worth $1.7 trillion dollars per year. According to the CIA world fact book, world GDP for 2006 was estimated at $65 trillion dollars[20] meaning oil accounts for over 2.6% of world GDP. It is a staggering amount of money for just one commodity. Further, the US consumed 20, 687, 410 of barrels of oil a day in 2006.[21] The US portion of that $1.7 trillion is over $501 billion dollars a year, just in oil. US oil purchases in 2006 rank just below the Netherlands estimated GDP (they rank twenty-sixth on the list).[22] That equates to enormous market power.

---

[18] "Annual Energy Report," Energy Information Administration, http://www.eia.doe.gov/aer/txt/ptb1105.html (accessed November 15, 2008).

[19] "Crude Oil Price History," New York Stock Exchange, http://www.nyse.tv/crude-oil-price-history.htm (accessed November 15, 2008).

[20] "Rank Order – GDP (Purchasing Power Parity)," 2006 CIA World Fact Book, http://www.umsl.edu/services/govdocs/wofact2007/rankorder/2001rank.html, (accessed March 3, 2009).

[21] "United States Energy Profile," Energy Information Administration, http://tonto.eia.doe.gov/country/country_time_series.cfm?fips=US (accessed March 3, 2009).

[22] 2006 CIA World Fact Book.

Oil has been seeping out of the ground for millennia. In ancient times, it was primarily used as a liniment for medicinal purposes. As time went on, it was also found that oil could be used as a source for lamp fuel and eventually machinery lubrication. Until a man named George Bissell arrived on the scene, oil was mainly thought of as a by-product of the many wells drilled for salt water or fresh water.

In the early 1850s, George Bissell conceived a plan to try and produce this oil commercially.[23] Bissell sent a sample to a chemist from Yale College named Professor Silliman who studied the sample and stated that "your company have in their possession a raw material from which . . . they may manufacture very valuable products . . . my experiments prove that nearly the whole of the raw product may be manufactured without waste, and this solely by . . . one of the most simple of all chemical processes."[24] With some financial backing, George Bissell formed the Pennsylvania Rock Oil Company and thus began the quest for oil. In 1859, a man named Edwin Drake began drilling the area near Titusville, Pennsylvania for the Pennsylvania Rock Oil Company. In August of that year, the Drake Well struck oil and they gathered twenty-five barrels of oil.[25] An industry was born and a 'black gold' rush ensued. Wells sprang up all over western Pennsylvania.

"Pennsylvania was responsible for one-half of the world's production of oil until the East Texas oil boom of 1901."[26] After oil finds in Texas, finds in Louisiana and California soon followed. Oil slowly began replacing whale oil and other animal fats to fuel lamps, until 1886

---

[23] "The Story of Oil in Pennsylvania," Paleontological Research Institution, www.priweb.org/ed/pgws/history/pennsylvania/pennssylvania.html, (accessed October 20, 2008).

[24] Ida Tarbell, *The History of The Standard Oil Company* (New York: McClure, Phillips, and Co, 1904), 7.

[25] Ibid, 10.

[26] Paleontological Research Institution.

when the German Engineer Karl Benz patented the first internal combustion engine which ran on gasoline which is a by-product of oil. Oil consumption has risen continually ever since.

Consider the invention of the Model T Ford. "In 1909 Henry Ford sold 10,660 cars …but by 1929 there were 23 million cars on the road – one for every five Americans."[27] Oil and the combustion engine led to the invention of the automobile and the automobile industry affected economic growth in a number of ways. The auto industry became the center for the application of mass-production techniques and was a stupendous source of employment – indeed the largest employer of the country.[28] The auto industry wasn't just the largest employer either. "It was the biggest customer for steel, rubber, sheet steel, lead, leather…and the largest industry in the nation."[29] The automobile and oil led to a rapid rise in growth that changed American life by increasing the number of families moving to the suburbs and vacationing became a national passion.[30] These profound economic, social, and physical changes to the nature of America also led to a mechanization of the armed forces and an ever increasing need for oil.

Oil uses further expanded when it was discovered that we could use oil to produce fertilizers, plastics, and synthetic rubber. We use it in our fertilizer to help grow the food and in our tractors to farm the food. We use plastics and various by-products of oil to ship and store the food and we transport the food all over the world via combustion engine transportation being run by fuel. Oil is ever-pervasive in our economy and our lives.

Oil was not only the fuel that turned the engine of America, oil also helped to drive the way businesses were organized as they started to grow vertically and horizontally. "The arch-

---

[27] Heilbroner and Singer, 261.

[28] Ibid.

[29] Ibid.

[30] Ibid.

example of successful vertical integration was the oil industry. Standard Oil began in 1870 as a refining company. Shortly thereafter it expanded "backward" into the actual drilling for oil, and it was also extended "forward" as a direct seller of products such as kerosene to the consumer.[31]

As stated earlier this is almost a two trillion dollar a year business. And this only accounts for the purchase of oil. It does not account for distribution or refinery profits or the fact that the volume of a barrel of oil is increased through the refinery process nor the literally thousands of products made from oil or the effects of oil on the 'transportation economy.' It is hard to find any other commodity in the world that has such an impact on the American economy and subsequently, the economy of the world. Oil has certainly elevated the standard of living for all Americans and helped fuel the economic growth of America for the last half century.

It was the convergence of oil and the combustion engine that transformed the economy of America. The continuing decline of oil production in America led to an increasing reliance on foreign oil. This, in turn, led US government and policy makers to be increasingly concerned about access to and the free flow of oil.

As one can clearly see, the impact of oil on our economy is considerable. Oil is a highly prized commodity as it affects the economic engine of America, and therefore the US way of life. It is omnipresent throughout society and has helped build the US into one of the great superpowers in modern time. Therefore oil has become extremely valuable to the US government and that value has led to increasing foreign policy initiatives into the Middle East to ensure the free flow of and access to oil.

The next chapter will provide a short history on the various national power elements that have been used to ensure the free flow of and access to oil. The focus for the reader is to

---

[31] Ibid, 177.

highlight some of the many ways that Presidents and policy makers have used elements of national power to maintain control over this vital commodity. In some cases, other elements of national power were used to secure the control of oil, in others, oil was the tool used to meet the US ends in the region. Oil has been a very successful tool and/or reason for leverage, market power, threat, coercion, and of course military action. These efforts helped to reshape the Middle East to where it currently stands today. The vital importance and realization of oil's increasing impact on our lives prompted the Standard Oil company to gain the approval to dispatch two geologists to Saudi Arabia in 1933. And thus began what would become the greatest oil bonanza in history.[32]

---

[32] Thomas Lippman, *Inside the Mirage: America's Fragile Partnership with Saudi Arabia* (Boulder: Westview Press, 2004), 27.

> **"We do not use oil for political purposes . . . Saudi Arabia also does not interfere in elections."**
>
> -Prince Abdullah

Chapter 3: Oil and National Power.

Daniel Yergin writes that "oil provided the point at which foreign policy, international economic considerations, national security, and corporate interests would all converge."[33] The importance of this chapter is to highlight the history of US involvement with Saudi Arabia and the greater Middle East and to understand that the concern of oil led us to the Middle East. However, the most important point to glean from this chapter is how oil was at the center of the great many foreign policy actions by the US in the Persian Gulf. Oil was not only the concern for US actions; it was also the means for some actions. The focal point of all this interest would be the Middle East and increasingly over time, Saudi Arabia. As Daniel Yergin also states:

> The lessons of World War II, the growing economic dependence on oil, and the magnitude of Middle Eastern Reserves all served, in the context of the developing cold war with the Soviet Union, to define the preservation of access to that oil as a prime element in American and British – and Western European – security.[34]

It is important to understand the context of events at the time US interest in the access to and the free flow of oil really began to rise. Within the period of just a little over 10 years, the US was attacked by the Japanese, declared war on Germany, and entered into a world war on two major fronts. After four years of fighting, the US won the war in Europe and also the war in Japan with the advent of the nuclear bomb. Within twenty-four hours after the victory in Japan, the US lifted gasoline rationing, which caused a demand that exceeded expectations.[35] Just a

---

[33] Yergin, 410.

[34] Ibid.

[35] Ibid, 409.

few short years later the US recognized the Jewish state of Israel. Added to all of this was the concern over the expansion of Communism by the Soviet Union immediately following World War II which led to publication by the National Security Council (NSC) of NSC-68 spelling out the United States foreign policy concept of 'containment.'

World War II to the 1960s:

Oil was paramount to the war effort and to the economic revival of America at the end of the war. Indeed, it was during World War II when political leaders and military strategists truly realized the importance of oil. It was not just economically important, it was militarily important, and it therefore became politically and strategically important. Military campaigns had as their primary objectives the seizure of oil fields. When Germany started their march into Russia in the winter of 1942 as part of Operation Barbarossa, one of their first objectives was to send Army Group South through the Russian steppes to the oil rich Caucasus region their goal was to seize the oil fields to starve the Russian Army of fuel and acquire those same resources for themselves. As Keith Miller stated in an article titled *"How Important was Oil?*

> The truth is--oil was the indispensable product, in all its forms, to the Allied campaigns around the world. Without it, World War Two could never have been won. For oil, once processed or refined in various ways, became the source of indispensable material for laying runways, making toluene (the chief component of TNT) for bombs, the manufacturing of synthetic rubber for tires, and the distilling into gasoline (particularly at 100-octane levels) for use in trucks, tanks, jeeps, and airplanes. And, that is not to mention the need for oil as a lubricant for guns and machinery.[36]

The recognition of the need for oil to fight the war became not only a tactical concern but also a strategic concern. Oil was the lifeblood to the machinery needed to fight the war. The growing realization of the need for oil militarily and economically, led to a greater role by the US in the

---

[36] Keith Miller, "How Important was Oil in World War II?" History News Network, http://hnn.us/articles/339.html, (accessed November 15, 2008).

Persian Gulf and specifically Saudi Arabia. Oil's importance led generals, strategic planners,

policy makers, and Presidents to ensure our access to oil.

It is from these concerns that the intertwined and mutually beneficial bilateral

relationship with Saudi Arabia began. A close look at the history of the two countries makes it

clear that oil is at the heart of the relationship. Strip away the excess and the relationship

between Saudi Arabia and the United States boils down to the following: the United States

needed access to oil and the strategic lines of communication that the Middle East afforded

during World War II, and Saudi Arabia needed our military security in a hostile region, access to

American money and global markets, and technical assistance for its burgeoning oil industry.

The rise of US and Saudi relations began in the early 1930s with US oil companies

searching for oil and was dramatically heightened during World War II by the concern over

access to oil. "The Franklin Delano Roosevelt presidency swung first toward land warfare not in

Europe proper but in North Africa."[37] While there are many reasons for the North Africa

campaigns of World War II, among them were concerns over securing the Suez Canal and access

to Middle East oil resources.[38] Strategic military planners and President Roosevelt understood

that the US needed access to Middle East oil and lines of communication through the region

during World War II. This led to a series of arrangements and the US reaching out to the Middle

East and specifically Saudi Arabia. Further: James F Byrnes, FDR's director of War

Mobilization testified that FDR "determined that in view of the strategic location of Saudi

Arabia, the important oil resources of that country…the defense of Saudi Arabia was vital to the

---

[37] Thomas Henriksen, "Is Leaving the Middle East a Viable Option?" *Joint Special Operations University* (08-1-2008): 11.

[38] Rick Atkinson, *An Army at Dawn, The War in North Africa, 1942-1943* (New York: Henry Holt and Company, LLC, 2002), 15.

defense of the United States."[39] Also at the time, the Secretary of the Interior, Harold Ickes repeatedly told the President, "Next to winning the war, the most important matter before us as a nation [is] the world oil situation."[40] The concern over oil became a concern at all levels of the government. These concerns led FDR to declare Saudi Arabia eligible for direct "lend-lease" economic assistance in February 1943, even though Saudi Arabia was a non-combatant.[41] As the British journalist David Holden wrote in his history of Saudi Arabia, "The great American takeover had begun."[42]

Additionally, FDR began correspondence with the king of Saudi Arabia, which eventually led to a meeting between FDR and the Saudi King Ibn Saud aboard the USS Quincy, just after the historic Yalta Conference in 1945. This was an incredibly historic meeting for both the US and Saudi Arabia, who had founded their country in 1932 after a series of military conquests between 1902 and 1926.[43] At this time, the modern kingdom of Saudi Arabia was 13 years old and had only discovered oil in 1938. And yet, Saudi Arabia was now on the world's stage, being courted by the British and the US, primarily because of their vast oil reserves. There are scant details on what was actually discussed between the two men. The bulk of the information comes from Colonel William A. Eddy who at the time was in charge of the US legation in Saudi Arabia and was present and interpreted for the King and FDR. Neither the joint memorandum nor Eddy's 1954 account of the meeting contain any specific agreements or

---

[39] Rachel Bronson, *Thicker Than Oil: America's Uneasy Partnership with Saudi Arabia* (New York: Oxford University Press, 2006), 24.

[40] Bronson, 39.

[41] Lippman, *Inside the Mirage*, 8.

[42] Thomas Lippman, "The Day FDR Met Saudi Arabia's King Ibn Saud," *The Link* 38, no. 2 (April-May 2005): 4 http://www.ameu.org/uploads/vol38_issue2_2005.pdf (accessed March 4, 2009).

[43] "Saudi Arabia: a chronology of the country's history and key events in the US-Saudi relationship," PBS Frontline, http://www.pbs.org/wgbh/pages/frontline/shows/saudi/etc/cron.html, (accessed February 13, 2009).

commitments by the United States or by Saudi Arabia, yet the impact of their afternoon together was far-reaching.[44] Colonel Eddy writes:

> The Guardian of the Holy Places of Islam, and the nearest we have to a successor to the Caliphs, the Defender of the Muslim Faith and of the Holy Cities of three hundred million people, cemented a friendship with the head of a great Western and Christian nation. This meeting marks the high point of Muslim alliance with the West," he wrote. The people of the Near East, Eddy added, "have hoped and longed for a direct dealing with the U.S.A. without any intervention of a third party. The habits of the past which led us to regard North Africa and the Near East as preserves of Europe were broken at one blow by Mr. Roosevelt when he met the three kings in the Suez Canal in 1945.[45]

Even though Roosevelt died shortly after the meeting, the friendship continued under Truman. The Export-Import Bank lent the Kingdom $10 million for public projects while the US Geological Survey agency sent a team to look for water and mineral resources and the American diplomatic mission in Jeddah was upgraded to full embassy status.[46]

Another critical aspect to note during this meeting between FDR and King Ibn Saud was the discussion of a Jewish homeland in Palestine. "In reply to Roosevelt's call for a Jewish homeland, the bitterly anti-Zionist Ibn Saud [King of Saudi Arabia] suggested that those displaced Jews who had somehow managed to survive the war be given a national homeland in Germany."[47] King Ibn Saud apparently was left with the impression from FDR that a Jewish homeland would not occur in Palestine under FDR's watch. Of course, all of that changed under Truman.

The end of World War II brought about many challenges for the US and chief among them were an expanding Soviet Empire, a call for isolationism from the American public and

---

[44] Lippman, "The Day FDR met Saudi Arabia's Ibn Saud," 11.

[45] Ibid, 12.

[46] Ibid.

[47] Yergin, 404.

some government officials, and a declining British Empire which ended its Palestinian mandate and revealed that it would no longer defend Greece and Turkey from Soviet aggression.[48] This left the US as the sole guarantor of any democratic strategic interest in the region against the rising Soviet Union. The Soviets also had significant interest in the Middle East because of the large oil reserves and their continuing quest for access to warm water ports. The US began its commitment to containing communism around the globe and this policy was articulated in NSC-68.

During the Truman tenure, the US and Saudi Arabia initiated a series of Agreements, including the US training of Saudi forces, the building of Dhahran Airfield and the "50/50 agreement." In return for the financial and military support, the king offered political backing for American activities in the region, exclusive of the Arab-Israeli conflict.[49] In 1950, President Truman wrote to inform King Saud that "No threat to your Kingdom could occur which would not be a matter of immediate concern to the United States."[50]

So grave was the concern of a Soviet takeover of the oil resources in the Middle East that the Truman administration detailed plans for the denial of Middle East Oil resources to hostile countries in a series of National Security Council documents. The NSC-26 series of documents spell out a directive from the Secretary of State to the Central Intelligence Agency (CIA) to "prepare a technical study of the question of plugging oil wells in Saudi Arabia."[51] The NSC-26 series of documents further lays out a viable plan for the denial of the oil fields with a

---

[48] Bronson, 44.

[49] Ibid.

[50] David Sandalow, *Freedom from Oil,* (New York: McGraw Hill, 2008), 186

[51] National Security Council. Directive 26/3, *Subject: Demolition and Abandonment of Oil Facilities and Fields in the Middle East*, June 29, 1950.

recommendation from the CIA to the Secretary of State to "include plans for plugging oil wells in Saudi Arabia."[52] "President Truman approved a detailed plan . . . to store explosives near Persian Gulf Oil Fields. As a last resort in the event of an imminent Soviet invasion, oil installations and refineries would be blown up and the reserves plugged to keep the oil out of Moscow's hands."[53] To show the extent of their concern it is important to note that also in NSC 26-3 the question of radiological means to prevent an enemy from utilizing the oil was discussed.[54] This plan ended up being rejected because "it could not prevent him [the enemy] from forcing 'expendable' Arabs to enter contaminated areas to open well heads and deplete the reservoirs."[55] However, "this calculation led to a strategy of using more conventional means to prevent the Soviets from seizing Persian Gulf oil . . . and explosives were moved to the region and stored near oil fields."[56]

One of the first major tests of the US and Saudi bilateral relationship occurred in the summer of 1948. The Jewish National Council proclaimed the state of Israel on May 14, 1948, and was immediately recognized by President Truman. A few days later, James Terry Duce, of the American owned oil company, Aramco, passed word to Secretary of State Marshall that King Ibn Saud had indicated that "he might be compelled, in certain circumstances, to apply sanctions against the American Oil concessions."[57] Ibn Saud further explained that it was "not because of his desire to do so but because the pressure upon him of Arab public opinion was so great that he

---

[52] Ibid.

[53] Shilbey Telhami and Fiona Hill, "Does Saudi Arabia Still Matter?" *Foreign Affaris* 81 (Nov/Dec 2002): 167.

[54] National Security Council 26/3.

[55] National Security Council 26/3.

[56] Telhami and Hill, 167.

[57] Yergin, 426.

could no longer resist it."[58] This was a crucial first test to the most egregious question that has

continually confronted the US and Saudi Arabian bilateral relationship. The response by King

Ibn Saud in 1948 also laid down an enduring concept between the two countries on the Arab-

Israeli issue that has lasted, in varying degrees, to the present day. There may be irreconcilable

differences over the Arab-Israeli issue between the US and Saudi Arabia, but realpolitik has

tended to prevail and the two nations will most likely work to find common ground on other

issues. Both countries share a pragmatic and mutual understanding on the need to maintain

relations and at the core of there relationship is oil. Consider King Ibn Saud's response to this

first test:

> When other Arab countries declared that Saudi Arabia should cancel the concession to
> retaliate against the United States and prove its allegiance to the Arab cause, Ibn Saud
> replied that oil royalties helped to make Saudi Arabia "a stronger and more powerful
> nation, better to assist her neighboring Arab states in resisting Jewish pretensions.[59]

Even though the Saudis vehemently opposed an Israeli state in Palestine since the beginning,

they have only felt it necessary to use their oil concession once, during the 1973 Arab-Israeli war

which will be discussed later. It is important to note that the arrangement of "oil for security"

between the US and Saudi Arabia has had a moderating effect on each country's policies since

the beginning.

> The Saudi and US governments' divergent responses to Arab-Israeli conflicts in 1948,
> 1967, and 1973 created conditions that severely tested bilateral relations. Nevertheless,
> the Truman, Eisenhower, Kennedy, Johnson, and Nixon administrations each viewed the
> Saudi monarchy as an ally in relation to other nationalist and socialist governments in the
> region and as a bulwark against the spread of Communism in the Gulf region and
> beyond.[60]

---

[58] Ibid.

[59] Ibid.

[60] Christopher M. Blanchard. Congressional Research Service report RL33533, *Saudi Arabia: Background and U.S. Relations,* May 22, 2008, 4.

What the author fails to mention is that oil was the underlying factor to maintaining relations even when they were severely tested. It is hard to deny that although there are major disagreements between the countries, oil is the "glue" that holds them together. Remove the oil and what bond is left?

Another tool of national power that President Truman and his administration used during his tenure was the "50/50" agreement. "Partly in response to its decision around Palestine, Washington sought ways to try to ease the pressure on its regional partners from angry critics. Toward Saudi Arabia in particular, the State Department looked for ways to increase economic support for the king."[61] In the aftermath of World War II and with a great deal of aid supporting the Marshall Plan, the Congress was unwilling to give out more foreign aid to another country. A precedent had been established a year earlier in Venezuela by "leveraging the American tax code which stipulated that a company operating in a foreign country could deduct the amount of taxes it paid to a host government."[62] This meant that Riyadh enjoyed increased profits and Aramaco paid no more taxes than the previous years as they was redirected to Saudi Arabia instead of the US.[63] Coinciding with this debate was the start of the Korean War, which again heightened concerns about the strategic vulnerability of oil, and the agreement was passed. As an example of increased profits, the US Treasury received $50 million in taxes from Aramaco while Saudi Arabia received $60 million in fees and royalties in 1950. In 1951, once the 50/50 agreement fully kicked in, Aramaco paid the US government $6 million while Riyadh received nearly $110 million.[64] This is another example of using oil to wield national power to achieve

---

[61] Bronson, 55.

[62] Ibid.

[63] Ibid.

[64] Ibid, 56.

your nations goals. It appears that Congress recognized this as well, for as late as twenty years later, "angry lawmakers accused Truman administration officials of using the 50/50 agreement to increase foreign aid to Saudi Arabia without Congressional consent."[65]

The major efforts to secure the free flow of and access to oil was formulated and implemented by FDR and Truman, and continued by Eisenhower. These were the years when the foundation of US foreign policy and our efforts in the Middle East were laid. Oil would continue to remain a strategic and vital concern for the US. In fact, the importance of oil would continue to increase as the US, for a variety of reasons, started to lose its capacity to produce oil even though its consumption rates continued to rise. It is important to note that through "the 1950s the United States produced nearly all the petroleum it needed. But . . . the gap between production and consumption began to widen and imported petroleum became a major component of the U.S. petroleum supply. Beginning in 1994, the Nation imported more petroleum than it produced."[66] As the Energy Information Agency article further states:

> Crude oil production in the lower 48 States reached its highest level in 1970 at 9.4 million barrels per day (Figure 12). A surge in Alaskan oil output at Prudhoe Bay beginning in the late 1970s helped postpone the decline in overall U.S. production, but Alaska's production peaked in 1988 at 2.0 million barrels per day and fell to just under 1.0 million barrels per day per well in 2000.[67]

Oil was certainly a strategic and vital concern for the US and therefore was a tool for policy makers and Presidents to wield as part of their concern for the American grand strategy and the pursuit of domestic and foreign policy objectives. However, it was clearly in the early

---

[65] Ibid.

[66] "History of Energy in the United States: 1635-2000," Energy Information Administration, http://www.eia.doe.gov/emeu/aer/eh/frame.html (accessed February 23, 2009).

[67] Ibid.

1970s when oil became a truly became a powerful weapon for use in the great game of geopolitics. Some may argue that this is where our overreliance on foreign oil really started, but the more critical question is what power would the US have been able to wield without oil?

1970s to Today:

The Nixon administration, and Henry Kissinger in particular, implemented the "Twin Pillars" policy in 1969 after a 1968 announcement that the British were going to withdraw from the Suez Canal.[68] Under the twin pillar policy, the United States left the security of the Persian Gulf to the region's most powerful states, Iran and Saudi Arabia.[69] At the time, Iran was the clear leader in the area by virtue of its large population, military might, geography covering the Straits of Hormuz and most importantly its leader, the Shah. With the Shah in charge, Iran was arguably the greatest ally to the United States in the Middle East at the time. Indeed, this was summed up in a May 1972 visit in Tehran between Nixon, Kissinger, and the Shah.[70]

> In two and one-half hours of conversations over two days, a deal was struck in which the United States agreed to increase the numbers of uniformed advisors in Iran and guaranteed the Shah access to some of the most sophisticated non-nuclear technology in the US military arsenal. The Shah, in return, agreed to accept a key role in protecting Western interests in the Persian Gulf region.[71]

The deal was struck in 1972 and was summed up at the end of the meetings when President Nixon told the Shah, "Protect me."[72]

---

[68] Gary Sick, *The Middle East and the United States: A Historical and Political Reassessment*, ed. David Lesch (Boulder: Westview Press, 2003), 292.

[69] R.K. Ramazani, "Security in the Persian Gulf," *Foreign Affairs* 57, no. 4 (Spring 79): 821 http://web.ebscohost.com/ehost/pdf?vid=9&hid=3&sid=560768d9-b355-47a9-b5ef-45ba688ef637%40sessionmgr7 (accessed January 23, 2009).

[70] Sick.

[71] Ibid.

[72] Ibid.

On October 17th, 1973 an oil embargo began when members of the Organization of Arab Petroleum Exporting Countries (OAPEC) decided that they would not ship their oil to the US and other countries that supported Israel during the Yom Kippur War. OAPEC consisted of members of the Organization of Petroleum Exporting Countries (OPEC), plus Egypt and Syria. This was in response to the US providing re-supplies to the Israeli military during the war. OAPEC decided to raise the price of oil and also reduce their supplies to those countries that they deemed had helped Israel during the Yom Kippur War. This caused widespread shocks around the globe with the price of oil quadrupling.

The 1973 Arab Oil embargo is an example of oil being used as leverage to make a political point. However, leverage works in either direction, so in response to OAPEC's actions, Henry Kissinger teamed up with the US Treasury Secretary, William E. Simon to lure American dollars back home.[73] "Kissinger believed that the only thing that could truly neutralize the oil weapon was heavy Saudi investment in the US economy, since an embargo that raised oil prices would only exacerbate American balance-of-payment problems, which would in turn hurt Saudi investments in the US economy."[74] A vital US commodity was leveraged into both economic and foreign policy interests, and was subsequently formalized in a *Joint Statement on Saudi Arabia-United States Cooperation.* "The Commission noted with interest that trade relations between the Kingdom of Saudi Arabia and the United States have been developing at an accelerated rate. U.S. exports to Saudi Arabia nearly doubled in 1971, increased by 40% in 1973, and nearly doubled again in 1974, to $835 million."[75]

---

[73] Bronson, 124.

[74] Ibid, 125.

[75] U.S. Department of State, *Joint Communiqué on the First Session of the U.S.—Saudi Arabian Joint Commission on Economic Cooperation, constituting an agreement on economic cooperation.* Done at Washington on 27 February 1975. Registered by the United States of America on 7 May 1976.

In one of the more bold examples of using oil as a tool for foreign policy, Andrew Scott Cooper espouses in an article how "in 1976, the US and Saudi Arabia colluded to force down oil prices, inadvertently triggering a financial crisis that destabilized Iran's economy and weakened the Shah's hold on power."[76] Using the declassified papers of Brent Scowcroft and transcripts of conversations between Nixon, Kissinger, Ford, and Simon, the article goes into great detail on how Treasury Secretary William E. Simon increasingly wanted to confront the Shah of Iran to help lower oil prices. "Skyrocketing oil prices had induced a deep recession in the United States, and for that reason alone Bill Simon had the Shah of Iran squarely in his sights."[77] "The Shah's refusal to join in the oil embargo had earned him a reputation as a statesman. But he also had engineered the December 1973 Tehran Oil Agreement that saw oil prices quadruple within 12 months."[78]

In a series of discussions over two years, Treasury Secretary Simon and Defense Secretary Ellsworth (and later Donald Rumsfeld) were urging both Nixon and Ford to confront the Shah and tell him to lower oil prices. Secretary of State Kissinger at first did not want to confront the Shah at all over this issue. Henry Kissinger considered the Shah "a tough, mean guy. But he is our real friend. He is the only one who can stand up to the Soviet Union. We need him for the balance against India."[79] Kissinger presciently added that "we can't tackle him without breaking him."[80] Kissinger was able to maintain his position over the course of two

---

[76] Andrew Scott Cooper. "Showdown at Doha: The Secret Oil Deal That Helped Sink the Shah of Iran." *The Middle East Journal* 62, no. 4 (October 1, 2008): 567-591. http://www.proquest.com/ (accessed February 17, 2009).

[77] Ibid.

[78] Hosain Razavi and Firouz Vakil, *The Political Environment of Economic Planning in Iran, 1971-1983* (Boulder: Westview Press, 1984), 63 as quoted in Cooper.

[79] Ibid.

[80] Ibid.

years but gradually began to realize that the Shah "was an ardent Persian nationalist who deeply distrusted the motives of his American admirers."[81] When President Ford called for reduced oil prices, the Shah responded that "no one can dictate to us. No one can wave a finger at us, because we will wave a finger back."[82] "By late 1976 the Shah was in deep financial trouble, facing a huge cash crunch. He wanted the Organization of the Petroleum Exporting Countries oil cartel, or OPEC, to raise oil prices by 25%, a move the U.S. opposed."[83]

Meanwhile, Secretary Simon was courting the Saudis to see what they could do. At first, the Saudis were reluctant to conduct such an action. However, coming to power after the death of King Faysal in 1975 was a group of men determined to use Saudi oil power as strategic leverage in improving relations with the US.[84] Saudi Arabia, as a primarily Sunni nation, and the Persian Shiites of Iran were invariably at odds with one another. Plus, at the time, Iran reigned supreme in the region and most importantly as the power player in OPEC, even though Saudi Arabia held the largest reserves of oil and held spare capacity allowing them to increase domestic output. Saudi Arabia wanted increased relations with the United States for security, arms, and military training and the Shah's insistence on raising oil prices (forced) President Ford into a position to collude with the Saudis.

"On Friday, September 17, 1976, Ford met with a second Saudi delegation. He explained that Western economies were gradually coming out of recession "but any increase [in the price

---

[81] Ibid.

[82] Yergin, 644.

[83] Borzou Daragahi, "U.S. policies led to Iran revolt, study says," *Los Angeles Times*, October 17, 2008. http://articles.latimes.com/2008/oct/17/world/fg-shah17 (accessed February 26, 2009).

[84] Cooper.

of oil] this December or for '77 would be extremely damaging."[85] Negotiations continued and

The Ambassador from Saudi Arabia, Ali Alireza, was invited to the White House on Monday,

November 29, 1976.[86] President Ford made it clear that he was concerned with the economy and

"he made it clear [to the Ambassador] that if Saudi Arabia wanted a strategic partnership with

the US it had to start acting like an ally. With friendship came responsibilities."[87]

Saudi Arabia responded even better than expected. Saudi oil minister "Yamani

announced that his government wanted no price increase at all for 1977" at the OPEC meeting

being held in Doha.[88]

> With the exception of the United Arab Emirates, the other members of OPEC ignored
> him and unanimously approved a 10% increase in the price of oil for January 1977 . . .
> Yamani stunned delegates with his response: Saudi Arabia would undercut the price
> offered by its competitors and boost its own domestic output from 8.6 million to 11.6
> million barrels of oil a day.[89]

At the end of the OPEC conference Yamani bluntly told reporters "We expect the West,

especially the United States, to appreciate what we did."[90] Kissinger was pleased with the

outcome at Doha telling Ford "we should get credit for what happened to the OPEC prices. I

have said all along the Saudis were the key."[91]

---

[85] Ibid.

[86] Ibid.

[87] Ibid.

[88] Ibid.

[89] Ibid.

[90] "Oil Price Rise Will Hold at 5%, Saudi Official Says," *Los Angeles Times,* December 18,
1976 as quoted in Cooper.

[91] National Security Adviser. Memoranda of Conversations, January 4, 1977, "Ford, Kissinger" as quoted in
Cooper.

It would quickly become a Pyrrhic victory for America as Iran was already over extended from massive military purchases and the Shah's Great Civilization programs were causing inflation to run rampant.[92] Cooper writes that "the collapse of the Doha summit, and the Saudi decision to undercut the price of Iranian crude and boost its output to try to flood the market, rushed the Iranian economy to the precipice."[93] The Shah's government responded by imposing strict budget controls that threw thousands out of work, collapsed investor confidence and panicked middle-class Iranians. Economic chaos and unemployment quickly spread.[94] Demonstrations in Iran followed within a year that eventually led to the downfall of the Shah.[95]

Mr. Cooper writes, "The Ford Administration, which had gone to great lengths to calculate the damage an increase in the price of oil would inflict on the American economy, apparently never attempted to measure the possible impact on the Shah and Iran's economy if the price rise did not go ahead."[96] This play of the oil weapon in the 'great game' of geopolitics is central to the argument that the vital interest over the control of oil needs a well thought out strategy. Too often policy becomes a short term solution absent any long term strategy and the immediate cure causes the patient to actually grow sicker.

Another example of oil and national power occurred in 2004 when Libya agreed to renounce terrorism and dismantle their weapons of mass destruction programs. What was considered a triumph of President Bush's American Policy in the region really came about more from Libya's need for revenue. "Last year [2002], a new prime minister, Shukri Ghanem, an

---

[92] Daragahi.

[93] Cooper.

[94] Daragahi.

[95] Ibid.

[96] Cooper.

economist, was appointed with an explicit reform agenda," in Libya.[97] Part of the agenda was

the Gaddafi regime's continuing goal to have the US sanctions lifted, which forced American oil

companies to leave the country in 1986.[98] With the lifting of sanctions, US oil companies would

be allowed back into Libya.[99] "Finally, on September 20, 2004, President Bush signed

Executive Order 12543 . . . paving the way for U.S. oil companies to try to secure contracts or

revive previous contracts for tapping Libya's oil reserves. The Order also revoked any

restrictions on importation of oil products refined in Libya, and unblocked certain assets."[100]

> The White House issued a press release stating that: "U.S. companies will be able to buy
> or invest in Libyan oil and products. U.S. commercial banks and other financial service
> providers will be able to participate in and support these transactions." On the same day,
> Libya's NOC [National Oil Company] announced its first shipment of oil to the United
> States in over 20 years.[101]

The American policy in the Persian Gulf under President George W. Bush may have had

some influence on Libya to renounce their WMD. But as the "largest holder of proven oil

reserves in Africa,"[102] Libya decided to renounce terrorism and WMD in order to open up their

oil economy for political survival.

While the bilateral relationship between Saudi Arabia and America has found common

ground on various issues confronting them through the years, the ability to cooperate during

times of mutual interest was formed because of the interrelationship of oil between the two

---

[97] George Joffe, "Why Gaddafi gave up WMD," BBC News, http://news.bbc.co.uk/2/hi/africa/3338713.stm (accessed February 23, 2009).

[98] Ibid.

[99] "Country Brief: Libya," Energy Information Administration, http://www.eia.doe.gov/cabs/Libya/Oil.html (accessed January 23, 2009).

[100] Ibid.

[101] Ibid.

[102] Ibid.

countries. More importantly, it was the common interest of oil during the times where the two countries disagreed that helped to have a moderating influence on their respective positions. At the heart of not ruining the relationship during these times of mutual disagreement were American concerns for oil and Saudi concerns for security and prosperity. Economically and diplomatically, the US ensured the free flow of and access to oil to support American interests. Oil was a tool to be used as leverage for agreements, alliances, economic trade, and to the downfall of the Shah. The importance of oil was so vital that it would concern the military use of national power as well.

Oil and Military:

Oil became the explicit military policy of the United States during the Carter administration. "In January 1980, the lingering fear generated by the [1973] embargo, combined with events such as the Iranian Revolution and the Soviet invasion of Afghanistan, led U.S. strategists to draw a line in the sand."[103] Deliberations over these current events made President Carter and the Joint Chiefs of Staff realize that their only options at the time were nuclear. This led to a series of initiatives to strengthen US resolve and access into the region, most of which are detailed in Presidential Directive/NSC-63, dated January 15, 1981. The subject of the directive from the NSC was the *Persian Gulf Security Framework*. In this declassified directive, the NSC laid out seven strategic themes "to defend our vital interests in the region"[104] and provided detailed guidance to the Departments of Defense, State, Treasury, Energy, and the Central Intelligence Agency.

---

[103] Steve Kretzman, "Oil, Security, War: The Geopolitics of U.S. Energy Planning," *The Multi-National Monitor* 24, no. 1 (Jan/Feb 2003): 13.

[104] National Security Council. Directive 63, *Subject: Persian Gulf Security Framework*, January 15th, 1981.

NSC-63 laid out broad strategic guidance to buildup US capabilities in the region to project force and maintain a credible presence; develop a broad range of military and related response options in and outside the region against the Soviet Union; and assist other countries in the region: to deter and diminish internal and external threats to stability, diminish radical influences. Further, the directive also wanted to improve access to facilities in the region and take a regional approach to securing [US] economic and political interest rather than basing their [Persian Gulf] nations defense wholly on drawing a line to protect specific countries in the region.[105]

The basic premise of NSC-63 was stated explicitly during the January 23, 1980, State of the Union address by President Jimmy Carter. President Carter stated, "let our position be absolutely clear: An attempt by any outside force to gain control of the Persian Gulf region will be regarded as an assault on the vital interests of the United States of America, and such an assault will be repelled by any means necessary, including military force."[106] This explicit comment on what we would do to protect oil in the Persian Gulf became known as the Carter Doctrine. The defense of the Persian Gulf now became the stated, explicit policy of the US. Oil was publicly proclaimed a 'vital interest,' to the United States. In the same speech Carter called for Congressional support for a 5% increase in real authorization for the Defense Department.[107] Just five weeks after the State of the Union address a: "Rapid Deployment Joint Task Force (RDJTF) was formally established at MacDill Air Force Base in Florida. By the time Ronald Reagan took office, the RDJTF included 100,000 Army troops, 50,000 Marines, and additional

---

[105] Ibid.

[106] U.S. President, Speech, "State of the Union Address," January 23, 1980, http://www.jimmycarterlibrary.org/documents/speeches/su80jec.phtml, accessed December 15, 2008.

[107] Ibid.

Air Force and Navy personnel. In January 1983, the RDJTF became the U.S. Central Command (USCENTCOM)."[108]

President Carter's administration laid out an enduring vision for the Persian Gulf that continues today. It was not only a vision; it was explicit guidance to the elements of national power about the US role in the Arabian Gulf. The Defense Department in particular not only stood up the RDJTF, they also endeavored to enhance their ability to 'force project' by increasing their operational reach into the region through strategic access to key countries, increasing their ability to utilize ships and planes, and staging forward-based equipment. The vision and guidance stated by President Carter was followed by President Reagan.

"Seven specific initiatives figured prominently in the Reagan administration's comprehensive effort to ramp up America's ability in the Persian Gulf."[109] All elements of national power were involved in the Persian Gulf expansion and access efforts. The RDJTF was upgraded to a full-fledged standing headquarters now known as US Central Command. The tiny island of Diego Garcia was turned into a major forward support base and the Defense Department established pre-positioned ships preloaded with large stocks of equipment. Construction and expansion of airbases and ports began throughout the Gulf region as well as negotiations over flight rights and agreements to permit US military access. There were increased efforts to cultivate client states through arms sales and training programs and finally, war plans were refined and military exercises occurred in the region on a regular basis.[110] Reagan increased defense spending dramatically. "Defense spending hit a peak of $456.5 billion

[108] Kretzman.

[109] Andrew Bacevich, "The Real World War IV," *Wilson Quarterly* 29, no. 1 (Winter 2005): 52 http://www.proquest.com/ (accessed February 17, 2009).

[110] Ibid.

in 1987 (in projected 2005 dollars), compared with $325.1 billion in 1980 and $339.6 million in 1981, according to the Center for Strategic and Budgetary Assessments."[111]

Military spending, combined with a concerted effort to increase the US military's ability to deploy into the region and have over flight and basing rights, greatly enhanced the US ability to respond to a crisis. This effort supplied the means to support President Carter's objectives from his State of the Union address in 1980. During this time Reagan and his chief advisers launched four operations into the Islamic world: Marines acting as peacekeepers in Lebanon, launching airstrikes against Libya, fighting the tanker wars of 1984-1988 and assisting Afghan freedom fighters throughout the 1980s.[112]

The 1990 invasion of Kuwait by Saddam Hussein and the potential for Saddam to also move into Saudi Arabia led to the Gulf War. The declassified National Security Directive 54 dated January 15, 1991 spells out in the first sentence that "Access to Persian Gulf oil and the security of key friendly states in the area are vital to U.S. national security."[113] It is important to note that such a directive would not be written lightly. Great care would have been taken for the development of such a directive as it circulated among the National Security Council which included Secretary of Defense Dick Cheney, Chairman of the Joint Chiefs of Staff Colin Powell, and Secretary of State James Baker, to name a few. Stating the 'Access to Persian Gulf oil' as the lead words in a directive of such magnitude underscores just how important oil is to the United States.

---

[111] Greg Schneider and Renae Merle, "Reagan's Defense Buildup Bridged Military Eras, Huge Budgets Brought Life Back to Industry," *Washington Post*, June 9, 2004. http://www.washingtonpost.com/wp-dyn/articles/A26273-2004Jun8.html, (accessed February 26, 2009).

[112] Bacevich, 47.

[113] National Security Council. Directive 54, *Responding to Iraqi Aggression in the Gulf,* January 15, 1991.

Of course military operations in the Persian Gulf region have continued to the present day with Operation Gothic Serpent in Somalia, Operations Desert Fox and Northern and Southern Watch, and Operations Enduring and Iraqi Freedom. These major actions in the Persian Gulf have signaled to the world the commitment by the United States to ensure the free flow of and access to oil. And this commitment is enjoyed by every other major oil importing nation in the world at great expense to the Americans.

Oil is certainly considered a vital commodity, worthy of exercising all elements of national power to ensure a reliable supply to continue to drive the economic engine of America. Oil has been a tool, a means, both directly and indirectly in the exercise of national power. Oil was the reason for strategic access, for security cooperation agreements, for arms sales, military training, basing and over flight rights. Diplomatically, oil provides a moderating influence on goals and objectives for both the producer and consumer. Oil enjoys a 2.6% share of the entire global commodity and therefore wields enormous economic power, both for the supplier and the consumer. Finally, oil is a national concern that warrants military force when threatened.

All of these policies, decisions, and events bring us to where we are today. The producers can use oil as leverage but so can the consumers. It is an intricate geopolitical dance that has as its heart the concern for oil. Oil as a vital interest led to the formulation of numerous policies to ensure the free flow of and access to oil. Oil has led to a mutually beneficial bilateral relationship between the US and Saudi Arabia. The US has achieved unprecedented access into a highly volatile region. The Saudis have maintained their hold on power in a country hampered with domestic dissent. Some may argue that this is exactly why the US needs to reduce their dependence on oil. In the long term, this may be true. However, in the short term, what is the cost of such a policy? As the US influence wanes, it is increasingly clear that China will assume the control. This process will occur over time, raising the chances of miscommunication and/or conflict over mutually competing goals between the US, Saudi Arabia, and China. Therefore, it is imperative that as the US begins to reduce its consumption of oil that we develop the right strategy, allowing us to unwind 60 years of policy, trade, agreements, and military force with minimum risk. In the next chapter we will discuss the numerous ways the US can reduce their consumption of oil.

**"If we force Western governments to invest heavily in finding
alternative sources of energy, they will"**

-former Saudi Oil Minister Sheik Yamani

Chapter 4: Reducing the dependence on foreign oil.

Sheik Yamani, the Saudi oil minister during the oil price shocks of the '70s and '80s, recognized the implications of a US reduction in oil consumption. After OPEC production cuts caused the price of crude to hit a record of $39.50 a barrel—roughly $100 a barrel in 2007 dollars, Sheik Yamani stated the quote above. He then followed it by "this will take them no more than 7 to 10 years and will result in their reduced dependence on oil as a source of energy to a point which will jeopardize Saudi Arabia's interests."[114]

"The United States imported about 58% of the petroleum which includes crude oil and refined petroleum products that we consumed during 2007. About half of these imports came from the Western Hemisphere. Our dependence on foreign petroleum is expected to decline in the next two decades."[115] These are the lead sentences from the US government's own website on Energy Information. The call to reduce our dependence on foreign oil has been steadily getting louder and louder over the last decade. The reasons are many but they generally fall into three main categories. One is that many experts predict that a "Peak Oil" production capacity will occur at some point in the next 5 to 25 years. The second is the growing concern over global warming theory and the hypothesized link between global warming and fossil fuels, and the final reason is the concern that America gives "petrodollars" to a growing host of countries who have interests inimical to the United States.

---

[114] John Cassidy, "The Coming Oil Crash," Conde Nast Portfolio, http://www.portfolio.com/views/columns/economics/2007/12/17/Why-Oil-Prices-Will-Drop (accessed January 10, 2009).

[115] "How Dependent Are We On Foreign Oil," Energy Information Administration, http://tonto.eia.doe.gov/energy_in_brief/foreign_oil_dependence.cfm (accessed January 15, 2009).

Whatever the reason, this clarion call really began with the 1973 Arab Oil embargo and, at least initially, a compelling case could be made that the concern fluctuated with the price of gasoline. However, since that time the concern about global warming, petrodollars, and peak oil has added to the argument for a reduction in the import and consumption of oil. The 1973 Arab Oil embargo spurred President Nixon into action and it was at this time that a drive for renewable energy began. On "November 7, 1973, President Nixon launched Project Independence, with the goal of achieving energy self-sufficiency by 1980. Recalling the Manhattan Project, Nixon declared that American science, technology, and industry could free the United States from dependence on foreign oil."[116] President Nixon also established the Energy Policy Office responsible for coordinating energy policies at the Presidential level.[117]

President Ford continued President Nixon's agenda of heightening energy concerns by signing the Energy Reorganization Act of 1974. The act began the consolidation of various departments and administrative staffs that dealt with energy under one umbrella. In 1975, President Ford signed the Energy Policy and Conservation Act which created a strategic petroleum reserve, extended the oil price controls and mandated automobile fuel economy standards.[118] President Carter continued along this path and established the Department of Energy in August 1977, giving a cabinet level position to the interests of energy.[119]

Concerns about energy independence waned for awhile due to a decrease in oil prices and energy concerns that were more focused on nuclear proliferation and technologies during Reagan and George H.W. Bush's presidencies.

[116] "Energy Timeline from 1971 to 1980," Department of Energy, http://www.energy.gov/about/timeline1971-1980.htm (accessed January 3, 2009).

[117] Ibid.

[118] Ibid.

[119] Ibid.

However, in 2005, President George W. Bush signed the Energy Policy Act of 2005 into law and he declared that "one day all Americans will look back on this bill as a vital step toward a more secure and more prosperous nation that is less dependent on foreign sources of energy."[120] The act focuses on four areas:

> First, we need to diversify America's Energy Supply through alternative renewable energies like wind, solar, and other technologies. Second, increase energy efficiency and conservation in our homes and businesses. Third, improve the energy efficiency of our cars and trucks through the use of ethanol and biodiesel with the goal of having 7.5 billion gallons per year of these fuels to offset fossil fuel. Finally, the fourth goal of the act is the need to modernize our electric power infrastructure.[121]

As a result of the Energy Policy Act of 2005, the federal government will spend $1.2 billion dollars on improving energy efficiency alone, excluding research and development funding. During this period as well, it will incur over $6.9 billion in lost revenue as a result of tax credits and deductions, including those provided for renewable energy.[122] Congress has been doing its part as well. The 110th Congress has initiated over 40 different bills for energy efficiency and renewable energy with about half of the bills focused on renewable fuels.[123]

Adding to federal incentives and spending, there have been very substantial private investment increases in the last few years. Venture capitalists invested over $1.7 billion in green technology in 2006 and surpassed that by 46% percent in the first three quarters of 2007, up to

---

[120] U.S. Department of Energy, *On the Road to Energy Security, Implementing a Comprehensive Energy Strategy: A Status Report,* Secretary Samuel W. Bodman, 1.

[121] Ibid.

[122] Susan Zinga, "What Does the Energy Policy Act of 2005 Mean for Energy Efficiency?" *Southface Journal* (Fall 2005): under "Research and Technology Transfer," http://www.southface.org/web/resources&services/publications/journal/sfjv305/sfjv305-energy_policyact_2005.htm (accessed January 18, 2009).

[123] Fred Sissine, Congressional Research Service report RL33831, *Energy Efficiency and Renewable Energy in the 110th Congress*, (2007), 2.

$2.6 billion.[124] According to data from Thompson Financial, venture capitalists have spent over $7 billion dollars on green technology since the year 2000.[125] Further adding fuel to this fire is former President Clinton who launched a $1 billion dollar investment fund for renewable energy in 2006, following multi-billionaire investor and businessman Richard Branson's pledge of $3 billion to combat global warming.[126] What began as a mainly economic issue in 1973 has now turned into an issue that spans all economic brackets, party affiliations, and world views.

> Fiscal hawks fret about the impact of growing oil imports on the dollar. Military types fear global conflict for dwindling resources in the event of catastrophic global warming. Neoconservatives worry about America's dependence on oil imports from unstable if not openly hostile countries in Latin America and the Middle East. Some think the solution is to simply pump more oil at home, but others argue that America needs to move away from oil altogether. One such figure, Jim Woolsely, former director of the Central Intelligence Agency, pointedly drives a Toyota Prius, a famously fuel-efficient car.[127]

And probably most surprisingly of all is that the major oil companies of the world have also started substantial research and development efforts into alternative energy sources. Exxon Mobil often touts its $100 million contribution to Stanford University's global Climate and Energy Project. By contrast, BP says it plans to spend $8 billion over the next decade developing alternative energy using wind, hydrogen and other means.[128]

---

[124] Jennifer Kho, "Greentech VC Hits $2.6B in U.S.," Greentech Media, http://www.greentechmedia.com/articles/greentech-vc-hits-26b-in-us-332.html (accessed January 15, 2009).

[125] "CleanTech Venture Investments by US Firms Break Record in 2007," PR Newswire, http://www.prnewswire.com/cgi-bin/stories.pl?ACCT=104&STORY=/www/story/11-28-2007/0004712795&EDATE (accessed January 15, 2009).

[126] Nahal Toosi, "Clinton Debuts $1B Renewable-Energy Fund," CBS News, http://www.cbsnews.com/stories/2006/09/22/ap/politics/mainD8KA10K00.shtml (accessed January 15, 2009).

[127] *The Economist*, Special Report: Waking up and catching up – Green America, January 27, 2007, 23.

[128] John Poretto, "ANALYSIS: Oil companies spending money on investments instead of new resources," *Missourian*, July 21, 2008. http://www.columbiamissourian.com/stories/2008/07/21/analysis-oil-companies-spending-money-investments-/ (accessed January 15, 2009).

Efforts to reduce US reliance on foreign oil have never been more substantial. Government, private industry, nation states, and the companies that are reaping the benefits from high oil prices are all investing in renewable energy and reducing our consumption of oil. Further, this has turned into a cultural issue as well. Recent polling suggests that across the range of renewable energy issues there are widespread majorities in its support. In a July 2008 poll, 64% of respondents think that finding new energy sources is important and 78% agree that the government should make fuel efficiency standards on cars stricter than they are now.[129]

The Case for a 20% Reduction in Oil Consumption:

There are numerous studies and plans today that lay out a strategy to reduce US consumption of oil. The plans incorporate many avenues and approaches that have at their heart a policy and/or technology solution. From a policy perspective, options include raising the corporate average fuel economy (CAFÉ) standards. One can also increase the gasoline tax to encourage a reduction in demand and utilizing the proceeds to fund other energy efficiency projects or institute a cap and trade program whereby producers are given a set amount of carbon emissions for a year and if they exceed that amount they have the option to try and trade for more carbon credits. A 2001 report demonstrated that by raising the CAFÉ standards for automobiles we could reduce oil imports by 11 percent in 2010 and by 27 percent in 2020.[130] Further policy options include a voucher or tax credit system to encourage the purchase of fuel efficient products and to provide large scale funding to renewable energy projects.

---

[129] "ABC News/Planet Green/Stanford University poll, July 23-28, 2008," Polling Report, http://www.pollingreport.com/energy.htm (accessed January 15, 2009).

[130] Howard Geller, "Strategies for Reducing Oil Imports: Expanding Oil Production vs. Increasing Vehicle Efficiency," American Council for an Energy Efficient Economy, http://www.aceee.org/pubs/e011.pdf (accessed January 11, 2009).

Technological options are many. Hybrid vehicle technology has already arrived, evident by the fact that more than 1,000,000 hybrid vehicles have been sold worldwide.[131] There is pursuit of clean coal, hydrogen power, biofuels, cars that burn natural gas, and cleaner burning diesel engines (since diesel engines are 30% to 40% more efficient than comparable gasoline engines).[132] Of course there is also wind and solar power for homes and businesses to reduce our consumption of home heating oil as well.

Achieving a 20% reduction in foreign oil in 10 years is easily within reach. The 2007 energy bill signed by President George W. Bush increases fuel-economy standards from 25 to 35 mpg as part of his "twenty in ten"[133] plan he announced during his 2007 State of the Union Address. The first step of that plan is to increase the supply of renewable and alternative fuels by the equivalent of 35 billion gallons by 2017, displacing 15 percent of projected annual gasoline use.[134] The plan also calls for "reforming and modernizing CAFÉ standards for cars" which would save an estimated "8.5 billion gallons" saving an additional 5 percent, for a total of 20% [reduction in gasoline use].[135]

President Obama and Vice President Joe Biden have gone further than any other Presidential administration on this issue, asking for $150 billion dollars alone to build a clean

[131] "Toyota Worldwide Hybrid Sales Top 1 Million Units," Toyota, http://www.toyota.co.jp/en/news/07/0607.html (accessed January 6, 2009.).

[132] Matt Vella, "Diesels Come Clean," *Business Week*, March 26, 2007. http://www.businessweek.com/autos/content/mar2007/bw20070326_220157.htm?chan=autos_autos+index+page (accessed January 6, 2009).

[133] Ann Compton, "Bush to Offer Bold Energy Plan," ABC News, http://abcnews.go.com/Politics/story?id=2816080&page=1 (accessed March 2, 2009).

[134] "Fact Sheet: Twenty in Ten: Strengthening Energy Security and Addressing Climate Change," The White House, President George W. Bush, http://georgewbush-whitehouse.archives.gov/news/releases/2007/05/20070514-2.html (accessed February 3, 2009).

[135] Ibid.

energy future.[136] According to a Congressional Research Service report, the federal government has spent $21 billion on the Manhattan Project, $96 billion on the Apollo program, and $115 billion on energy research and development efforts in 2007 dollars.[137] The Obama-Biden plan would surpass in one bill the combined federal spending for energy research and development over the last 35 years. They are well on their way and have adopted many of the programs, incentives, and policies listed above. In the first Obama Stimulus bill just passed, energy received "about $38 billion in government spending and about $20 billion in tax incentives over the next 10 years, according to estimates.[138] Covered in the bill are programs for battery technology, improved electricity grids, tax credits to purchase a plug-in hybrid vehicle and for wind and solar energy programs, and battery technology, to name a few. It is safe to say that it was the single largest amount of money allocated to energy spending in the history of the United States.

Additionally, President Obama has signed an executive order accelerating the 2007 CAFÉ standards by allowing "California and 13 other states, representing about 50 percent of the U.S. automobile market, to force carmakers to meet the 35.7 mpg standard by 2016, rising to 42.5 mpg in 2020."[139] President Obama has accelerated the 2005 Bush Energy Bill with the signing of his Executive Order and the passing of the American Recovery and Reinvestment Act (2009 Stimulus Bill) containing $58 billion in spending or tax credits for energy programs.

[136] "Energy and the Environment," the White House, President Barack Obama, http://www.whitehouse.gov/agenda/energy_and_environment/ (accessed January 18, 2009).

[137] Deborah D. Stine, Congressional Research Service Report RL34645, *The Manhattan Project, the Apollo Program, and Federal Energy Technology R&D Programs: A Comparative Analysis,* (2008), 1. The dollar amounts expressed here cover the total spending over the life of the programs and have been adjusted to 2007 dollars.

[138] Martin LaMonica, "Obama signs stimulus plan, touts clean energy," cnet news, http://news.cnet.com/8301-11128_3-10165605-54.html (accessed March 2, 2009).

[139] "From peril to progress (Update 1: Full Remarks)," the White House, President Barack Obama, http://www.whitehouse.gov/blog_post/Fromperiltoprogress/ (accessed February 3, 2009).

The salient point here is not in the many ways the US can decrease their dependence on foreign oil but rather on the fact that it can be done, efforts are underway, and there certainly seem to be more to follow. There are feasible, acceptable, and suitable efforts underway that will lead to a 20% reduction in oil consumption, so we consider the broad effects that might entail. President Obama has a stated goal to "save more oil than we currently import from the Middle East and Venezuela combined."[140] Since "Middle East" can have varying definitions, this paper will consider the Middle East as OPEC.[141] In 2007, the US consumed 20.68 million barrels of oil per day and OPEC provided 2.115 million barrels of oil per day, accounting for 10% of the oil consumed by Americans.[142] During 2007, two of the five largest countries we imported our oil from were Saudi Arabia at 11% and Venezuela at 10.1% of the total imports.[143] As stated earlier, the average price for a barrel of oil in 2006 was $66.43. That price, multiplied by 2.1 million barrels of oil a day for a year equals almost $51 billion dollars a year in revenues from a 10% reduction in oil. A 20% reduction in oil would equal over $102 billion dollars. $102 billion dollars is larger than the GDP of over 161 countries.[144] In fact, $102 Billion would rank as number 68 out of the 229 countries on the list.[145] A 20% reduction in oil by the US is equal to a larger GDP than the vast majority of countries on the list. According to the CIA world fact book, in Saudi Arabia, "the petroleum sector accounts for roughly 80% of budget revenues,

---

[140] "New Energy for America," Barack Obama and Joe Biden, http://my.barackobama.com/page/content/newenergy (accessed January 18, 2009).

[141] Organization of Petroleum Exporting Countries currently consists of the countries of Algeria, Angola, Ecuador, Indonesia, Kuwait, Iran, Iraq, Libya, Nigeria, Qatar, Saudi Arabia, United Arab Emirates, and Venezuela.

[142] "U.S. Imports by Country of Origin," Energy Information Administration, http://tonto.eia.doe.gov/dnav/pet/pet_move_impcus_a2_nus_ep00_im0_mbbl_m.htm (accessed January 15, 2009).

[143] Ibid.

[144] "Rank Order - GDP (purchasing power parity)," Central Intelligence Agency, The World Fact Book, https://www.cia.gov/library/publications/the-world-factbook/rankorder/2001rank.html (accessed March 2, 2009).

[145] Ibid

45% of GDP, and 90% of export earnings" and their GDP was estimated at $600 Billion in 2008.[146] A $100 billion dollar reduction in the oil market in a country whose GDP was estimated to be at $600 billion (45% from their petroleum sector), would be a serious concern for the Saudis. It is an enormous amount of influence which would increasingly be lost as the US transitions away from oil.

So far we have discussed why oil is considered a vital resource and highlighted the varying ways in which Presidents and policy makers have ensured that the US maintains the free flow of and access to oil through alliances, agreements, trade, and military means. If oil is indeed a vital commodity that has necessitated numerous diplomatic, economic, and military actions for over 60 years, one has to follow the logic that lessening the need for oil carries with it strategic risks. Oil has led to alignments and relationships between countries, helped to ensure strategic access to regions, maintain the global commons, and facilitate numerous bi-and multilateral economic and security arrangements between countries. Implicitly and explicitly oil has been a means to achieve national goals. While we cannot change the past, reviewing the last 60 years can help to ensure that before we begin the process of reducing the US consumption of foreign oil that we develop the correct strategy for moving forward.

This paper postulates a gradual reduction off oil consumption as the US transitions to a renewable or alternative energy economy. However, it needs to be mentioned that this could obviously occur more slowly, which is easier, in most respects, to absorb. More importantly, however, is the fact that the timeline could move more quickly with a breakthrough technology. Remember that in 1909 Ford sold over 10,000 cars but just 20 years later, there were 23 million

---

[146] "Saudi Arabia," Central Intelligence Agency, The World Fact Book, https://www.cia.gov/library/publications/the-world-factbook/geos/sa.html (accessed March 2, 2009).

cars on the road, one for every five Americans.[147] In twenty years America was transformed. If something like this occurs with renewable energy, Presidents, policy makers, and strategists will need to cautious as a quickened pace for the reduction of renewable energy would only exacerbate the potential geopolitical fallout. Countries whose GDPs are largely funded by oil exports will being to collapse.

We now turn to China and their spectacular rise onto the world stage.

---

[147] Heilbroner and Singer, 261.

Chapter 5: China.

To have an idea of how a US reduction in the consumption of foreign oil and the growth of China may impact the Middle East and Saudi Arabia, we must remember the goals, pursuits, and interests of America in the last sixty years in the same region. As the US assumed the mantle of leadership during World War II, the dominant power in the Middle East was Britain. America assumed this role and, as discussed earlier, began foray after foray into the Middle East with the overarching goal the free flow of and access to oil to support the economic engine of America. Are we now at a strategic crossroads where China will take the reign?

China is an industrial nation on the rise with a growing middle class, leading to a growing demand for resources. China's power is growing rapidly and its economy expands at about 10 percent annually.[148] "China is poised to have more impact on the world over the next 20 years than any other country. If current trends persist, by 2025 China will have the world's second largest economy and will be a leading military power."[149]

The rise of China has been a remarkable event in the course of human history. "It took the British just under 60 years and the US and Japan about 40 years to double their respective gross domestic product. It took China all of 12 years."[150] China has been the world's fastest growing economy in the past quarter century, and as such, its appetite for energy has grown rapidly. "China's energy needs are growing faster than any other country."[151] This has led, in

---

[148] Jeffrey A. Bader and Richard C. Bush III, "Contending with the Rise of China, Three Decades of Progress," in *Opportunity 08, Independent Ideas for America's Next President,* Michael E. O'Hanlon, editor, (Washington D.C.: Brookings, 2007), 38.

[149] United States National Intelligence Council, *Global Trends 2025: A Transformed World,* (Washington DC: US Government Printing Office, 2008), 29. Hereafter cited as *Global Trends 2025.*

[150] Gabor Steingart, *The War for Wealth* (New York: McGraw Hill, 2008), 5.

[151] "China's Thirst for Oil," *International Crisis Group* (9 June 2008): i http://www.ciaonet.org/wps/icg/0001342/0001342.pdf (accessed February 23, 2009).

the last ten years, to China moving from a petroleum exporter to the second largest oil importer in the world after the United States.[152] Further, forecasts predict that Chinese demand for crude will increase by 12% annually until 2020.[153] "The broader picture is alarming: if every 1.3 billion Chinese were to use 20 times more energy everyday, i.e. the per capita consumption as in North America, China would require 80 million barrels of oil a day – more than the entire world's daily consumption."[154]

China's quest for energy has invariably led it to the Middle East. China became a net oil importer in 1993 and was receiving 1.2% of its imported oil from Saudi Arabia, but by 2005, China received 17.5% of its imported oil from the Saudis.[155] China has made significant inroads into Saudi Arabia. In 2008, China imported 36 million metric tons of oil from Saudi Arabia, the most of any country.[156] China has also made extensive business deals with Saudi Arabia, including joint ventures between both state owned oil companies to search for gas deposits in Saudi Arabia, and providing engineering services to two refineries in the kingdom.[157]

The rise of China's economy has also brought about the rise of the Chinese military – the People's Liberation Army (PLA).

> If GDP alone directly translated into military power, in the 2030s China would have the capacity to afford military forces equal to or superior to current US capabilities. And

---

[152] Wenran Jiang, "China's Quest for Energy Security," *The Jamestown Foundation* 4, no. 20 (October 14, 2004): 2 http://www.ciaonet.org/pbei-2/jfcb/jfcb_v4_20/jfcb_v4_20.pdf (accessed February 12, 2009).

[153] Ibid.

[154] Jiang.

[155] Steven Yetiv and Chunlong Lu, "China, Global Energy, and the Middle East," *The Middle East Journal* 61, no. 2 (Spring 2007): 203.

[156] Winnie Zhu and Wang Ying, "Sinopec, Aramco May Agree on Oil Supply, Refinery (Update1)," Bloomberg.com, http://www.bloomberg.com/apps/news?pid=20601207&sid=a0QhDUVADLJg&refer=energy (accessed March 9, 2009).

[157] Ibid.

while one must temper such calculations by per capita measures . . . by the 2030s China could modernize its military to reach a level of approximately one quarter of current US capabilities without any significant impact on its economy.[158]

The Chinese have undertaken programs to expand their military that is consistent with the classical Chinese strategic thinkers incorporating intelligence, submarines, cyber, and space.[159] Additionally, the Chinese have undergone a "renaissance in military thinking . . . that draws on the classics of Chinese writings and an extensive examination of Western literature on history, strategy, and war."[160]

Figure 1: Chinese Defense Budget and Estimates of Total Defense-Related Expenditures.[161]

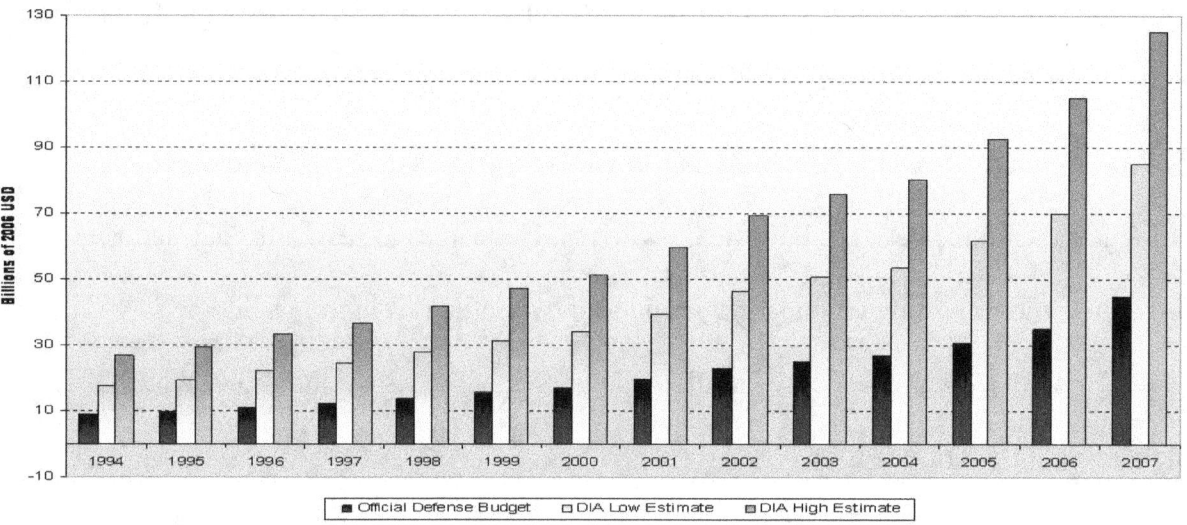

As the graphic illustrates, statistics on the exact amount China is spending on their military are hard to come by. A recent 2008 announcement by the Chinese stated that they will increase their military spending for the year with a 17.6 increase (roughly equal to last year's increase and

---

[158] U.S. Joint Forces Command, *The Joint Operating Environment 2008, Challenges and Implications for the Future Joint Forces,* November 2008, 27. Hereafter cited as *Joint Operating Environment 2008.*

[159] Ibid, 27.

[160] Ibid.

[161] U.S. Department of Defense, Annual Report to Congress, *Military Power of the Peoples Republic of China 2007,* 27.

giving them a $59 billion dollar defense budget).[162] However, as the graphic shows, the US has

long been suspicious of China's numbers. Further, China's emphasis on nuclear submarines

underscores worries that the United States possesses the ability to shut down China's energy

imports of oil – 80% of which go through the Straits of Malacca.[163] "China's growing interest

and influence from the South China Sea through the Indian Ocean and on to the Arabian Gulf

has been described as a 'String of Pearls' approach that potentially could present the United

States with complex regional challenges."[164]

Figure 2: Chinese political influence or military presence astride oil routes.[165]

As seen in the graphic, China has continued to expand the operational reach of its navy, focusing

on the trade route from the Middle East to China. In 2001, "China has clinched a deal to develop

a major deep-sea commercial port in western Pakistan, giving Beijing a potential staging ground

---

[162] "Chinese to boost military spending again in 2008." *Chicago Tribune,* March 5, 2008, http://www.proquest.com/ (accessed March 3, 2009).

[163] *Joint Operating Environment 2008,* 27.

[164] Christopher J. Pherson, *String of Pearls: Meeting the Challenge of China's Rising Power Across the Asian Littoral,* Strategic Studies Institute, Carlisle Barracks, July 2006.

[165] *Joint Operating Environment 2008.* The statement "String of Pearls" is sourced from Christopher Pherson, "Meeting *the Challenges of China's Rising Power,"* footnote above.

to exert influence along some of the world's busiest shipping lanes flowing into and out of the Persian Gulf."[166] This is the Gwadar Naval Base that is located on Pakistan's western border astride the entrance to the Straits of Hormuz. The article from 2001 goes on to explain that:

> China's role at Gwadar echoes similar concerns voiced when a Hong Kong firm with close ties to China's communist leadership won the leases to two ports near both ends of the Panama Canal in 1997. Clinton and Bush administration officials have said they have seen no interference by China in the operation of the canal, but a U.S. intelligence report in October 1999 called the leases "a potential threat" to U.S. interests.[167]

As an example of what may occur in the Middle East, we can look at what has recently happened to US efforts in South America. In 1999, the US signed a ten year lease with Ecuador for use of the Manta Air Base by US Southern Command as a location for use by the Joint Interagency Task Force in their fight against drugs.[168] Ecuador informed the United States in July 2008 that it will not renew the lease for Manta Air Base when it expires in November 2009.[169] Further, Ecuador offered the same base to China.[170]

With China's increasing economic and military rise in the region, it is clear that the Chinese have studied their history well. China has been able to befriend every nation in the Middle East in some fashion, to include Iran and Israel. The primary reason is that China does not bring with them any "good governance requirements, human rights conditions, approved-project restrictions, and environmental quality regulations that characterize U.S. and other

---

[166] David R. Sands. "China suspected in port deal Beijing naval vessels expected to dock at Pakistani site: [2 Edition]." *Washington Times*, May 31, 2001, http://www.proquest.com/ (accessed March 3, 2009).

[167] Ibid.

[168] "China, Ecuador: Beijing's Latin American Opportunity," Stratfor, http://www.stratfor.com/analysis/china_ecuador_beijings_latin_american_opportunity (accessed March 3, 2009).

[169] "Background Notes, Ecuador," U.S. Department of State, http://www.state.gov/r/pa/ei/bgn/35761.htm (accessed March 5, 2009).

[170] Stratfor.

Western government investments."[171] Practitioners of realpolitk are proud. The Chinese are only concerned about secure oil supplies.

The expansion of China economically and militarily is clearly on the rise. Chinese concerns over oil revolve around access to and the free flow of oil to their country and concern over any American effort to interrupt the flow. History has shown that the US had similar goals in the same region, only the American's concerns were with the Soviets. The Chinese would prefer to see the US begin a major program to reduce its dependence on oil that would further degrade any US influence into the region, allowing China's further entrenchment in the Persian Gulf. The overarching goal of ensuring the free flow of and access to oil to help fuel a growing and expanding economy could lead down the same well-traveled paths already worn by the US. There are many signs that the Chinese review the US efforts in many endeavors to learn from what worked and correct what did not. "One of the fascinating aspects of China's emergence over the past three decades has been its efforts to learn from the external world."[172] China, in many respects, is in roughly the same position as the US was 70 years ago. Before we begin the confluence of events, the next chapter will detail Saudi Arabian concerns.

---

[171] Kerry Dumbaugh, Congressional Research Service Report RL 34588, *China's Foreign Policy: What Does It Mean for U.S. Global Interests?*, dated July 18, 2008, 12.
[172] *Joint Operating Environment 2008, 28.*

"So complex and sensitive is the US-Middle East relationship that every development of consequence affecting the area always lands on the President's desk."

-Andrew Killgore

Chapter 6: Saudi Arabian concerns.

Saudi Arabia plays a significant role in any country that has a concern over the free flow of and access to oil. Saudi Arabia sits on the largest oil reserves in the world and has the largest spare capacity enabling them to respond quickly to any oil interruptions. As the holder of the largest reserves and spare capacity, they also wield the most power in OPEC. Saudi Arabia is also the birthplace to Islam and home to the two holiest sites in Islam – Mecca and Medina.[173] Guaranteeing the security of Saudi Arabia has been the United States which, as detailed earlier, has had large scale diplomatic, economic, and military efforts in the region. The US has invested both economically and militarily with Saudi Arabia since their relationship began.

> From 1950 through 2006, Saudi Arabia purchased and received from the United States weapons, military equipment, and related services through Foreign Military Sales (FMS) worth over $62.7 billion and foreign military construction services (FMCS) worth over $17.1 billion (figures in historical dollars). These figures represent approximately 19% of all FMS deliveries and 85% of all FMCS deliveries made worldwide during this period. The largest single recent U.S. foreign military sale to Saudi Arabia was a $9 billion contract for 72 F-15S fighter aircraft.[174]

Additionally, and perhaps more importantly to Saudi Arabia, has been the explicit guarantees made by successive Presidents through the years that Saudi Arabian security was a concern of the United States.

"After the creation of the present Kingdom of Saudi Arabia, the central security concern of its founder and first ruler was the preservation of the Kingdom's very existence."[175] "By a shrewd strategy and policy, Ibn Saud was able to enlist the British to contain the Hashemite

---

[173] "Saudi Arabia," Central Intelligence Agency, The World Fact Book.

[174] Blanchard, 16.

[175] Nadav Safran, *Saudi Arabia, The Ceaseless Quest for Security,* (Ithaca: Cornell University Press, 1985), 71.

threat during the lean years before oil revenues began to flow, when the internal situation was precarious. When the British became less able or willing to continue in that role, at least in Ibn Saud's eyes, he tried to use his newly acquired oil wealth to obtain a security guarantee from the United States, gain diplomatic allies and friends among Arab leaders opposed to the Hashemites, and build up armed forces and instruments of security for purposes of internal and external deterrence.

Today, Saudi Arabia's two biggest threats in the region are Iran and Iraq. They are natural rivals for power and influence in the Gulf and the struggle to preserve the balance of power in the region requires a constant Saudi effort to balance Iran and Iraq.[176] Iran has never been considered a friend to the Saudis and in recent years Iran has become even more of a concern. "There is considerable nervousness inside the kingdom about both Iran's nuclear program and its regional ambitions."[177] And the Saudis, in many respects, feel like the US is handing Iraq to Iran on a silver platter.[178]

Saudi Arabia also deals with a growing dissent among its population. The Saudis have dealt with the radical Islamists for some time by funding Wahabbi schools throughout the world. These efforts came under intense scrutiny after the events of 9/11 when it was discovered that 15 of the 19 hijackers were of Saudi Arabian descent. Since 9/11 the US has been putting increasing pressure on the Saudis to help quell radical Islam and terrorism. Saudi Arabia has

---

[176] Anthony Cordesman, "Saudi Arabia Enters the Twenty-First Century: The Political, Foreign Policy, Economic, and Energy Dimensions," *Praeger Security International* (2003): under "Iran and Iraq: The Primary Threats," http://psi.praeger.com/doc.aspx?newindex=1&q=Saudi+Arabia+security+concerns&c=&d=/books/dps/200094ab/200094ab-p200094ab9970041001.xml&i=1#txmlhit (accessed March 11, 2009).

[177] Rachel Bronson, "What Saudi Arabia Wants - Good Neighbors," Saudi-US Relations Information Service, http://www.saudi-us-relations.org/articles/2007/ioi/070417p-bronson-neighbors.html (accessed February 25, 2009).

[178] "Saudi Arabia: Feeling the Iranian Pinch in Iraq," STRATFOR, http://www.stratfor.com/saudi_arabia_feeling_iranian_pinch_iraq (accessed February 11, 2009).

responded with the abduction of terrorists in their country. However, the fact remains that the Islamists have clearly been the most articulate and powerful of the various social forces in Saudi Arabia.[179] This has had some spillover effects as well in the Arab world, which is troubling to the Saudis. Frequently "Hizballah, Syria and Iran have used Saudi and Egyptian ties with the United States to discredit Riyadh and Cairo as champions of Arab and Muslim causes."[180]

All of these factors have slowly led to Saudi Arabia wanting to assume a more independent role in its own security.[181] In 2007, Saudi Arabia brokered a deal between Fatah and Hamas and hosted an Arab League Summit which they had declined to attend the two previous years. Also in 2007, King Abdullah also hosted Iran's President Ahmadinejad and canceled a state dinner with President Bush.[182] Recently Saudi Foreign Minister Prince Saud al-Faial warned Iran on two separate occasions to stop meddling in inter-Arab affairs and has urged Arabs to unify clearly concerned with Iranian efforts to acquire nuclear weapons.[183] Additionally, this has brought about a renewed emphasis by the Saudis to acquire from Pakistan both Chinese-designed missiles and dual-key Pakistani nuclear warheads which is a major concern by the US.[184] Saudi Arabia is now flexing their muscle in the Middle East and has taken an increasing role in managing their own affairs. This scenario could lead to either cooperation

---

[179] Gwenn Okruhlik. "Networks of dissent: Islamism and reform in Saudi Arabia." *Current History* 101, no. 651 (January 1, 2002): 22-28. http://www.proquest.com/ (accessed March 11, 2009).

[180] Steven A Cook. (2008). Disentangling Alliances: America in the Middle East. *The American Interest, 4*(1), 86. Retrieved March 11, 2009, from ProQuest Social Science Journals database. (Document ID: 1544727731).

[181] Simon Henderson, "Chinese-Saudi Cooperation: Oil but also Missiles," The Washington Institute for Near East Policy, http://www.ciaonet.org/pbei/winep/policy_2006/2006_1095/2006_1095.html (accessed February 12, 2009).

[182] Bronson, "What Saudi Arabia Wants – Good Neighbors"

[183] Salah Hemeid, "Not at our expense," *Al-Ahram Weekly (Cairo,)* April 1, 2009. http://weekly.ahram.org.eg/2009/940/re81.htm (accessed April 1, 2009).

[184] Ibid.

or competition between the US and China in the region. Further, in this scenario, Saudi Arabia will increasingly align with the countries who are buying their oil. A geopolitical shift will begin with the rise of China in the Persian Gulf region secondary to a diminishing American presence, which will intensify Saudi Arabian concerns for their security.

> **"Contexts of conflict and war are the environment created by the confluence of major trends. Contexts illuminate why wars occur and how they might be waged."**
>
> **-Colin Gray**

Chapter 7: Confluence of Events.

Oil is power, leverage, a reason, or an excuse to exercise and wield elements of national power to ensure that the country has their energy needs. The US has used the concern for oil, the market power of oil, and their military power to control oil for the last 60 years. We have discussed in detail the increasing economic, diplomatic, and military actions that the US has undertaken to ensure their access to and the free flow of oil. Meanwhile, China is on the rise, growing faster than any other nation and with this growth an increasing demand for oil. China is also now concerned with the free flow of and access to oil, which has led to increasing efforts to secure oil guarantees from the countries in the Middle East. As once the biggest producer of oil and always the biggest consumer, the US has wielded their oil power often and to great success, and admittedly in some cases, peril.

The confluence of a decreasing need of oil and therefore decreased market power from the US and a growing thirst from China leads to a diminishing US role and an increasing Chinese one. In the middle, between of these two powerful countries, is Saudi Arabia. Saudi Arabia will take note of the United States shift to renewable energy programs from the numerous policies and funds being committed. At the same time, they will see a growing China, the manufacturer of the world, and its increasing needs for oil. The Saudis will begin to question how long the US might be willing to continue to provide for their security in the region when the US no longer needs their oil. Oil, trade, and resources will begin to shift from a US-Saudi Arabia relationship to a Saudi Arabia-China relationship. In this scenario, the US is increasingly left out as their market power dwindles, leaving them with fewer options to exercise national power in the region while the Chinese make more and more inroads into the region. Meanwhile, China continues to grow economically at a dizzying rate, requiring more power and as a result, more oil. China will thereby increase their dependency on foreign oil. "From a practical standpoint, China shifted from a net oil exporter to a net oil importer in 1993."[185] There is growing concern and effort by the Chinese to ensure their oil security for the future and they correctly consider that the biggest threat to their security is the United States.[186]

Further, as the US continues to reduce its dependence on oil, Presidents, policy makers, and the populace will begin to ask if the US really needs a large scale military presence in the Persian Gulf and whether or not the US should continue to provide security for Saudi Arabia and other allies in the region. "No blood for oil," is a rallying cry often heard in protest of US military engagements in the Persian Gulf, but it never amounted to a clarion call that mustered large scale protests like the US witnessed during the 1960s and the Vietnam war. Americans intuitively knew that there was great need for oil as they got into their SUVs to drive to the grocery store. However, "no blood for oil" would take on an entirely different meaning in a US where everyone drives a hybrid, electric, or natural gas vehicle. As Colin Gray states, "all policy and strategy is made at home. It will be influenced, perhaps triggered, sometimes dominated, by external considerations, but the making, administration, and execution of policy and strategy is a process embedded in the culture of domestic context."[187]

It seems that history repeats itself, only with different characters. The British once played the role of the great superpower up until World War II. At the time, the British had

---

[185] Erica Downs, "China's Quest for Energy Security," *Rand Corporation* (2000): 12 http://www.rand.org/pubs/monograph_reports/MR1244/ (accessed February 23, 2009).

[186] Ibid.

[187] Gray, 90.

occupied many colonies throughout the Near East, and indeed, the world. Due to a variety of events but mainly the effects of World War II, the British decided to pull out of their colonies in the Near East. Luckily for the Western World, the US was able to assume the mantle of leadership in the region. At the time, the Saudis preferred the US to the British since they did not bring any colonialist designs (or stipulations) to the region and only wanted oil. A mutually beneficial bilateral relationship revolving around oil has ensued to the present day.

Today, in many regards, the US is in the same position that the British were in post World War II. This time however, the Chinese are set to win, which should be a big concern for the western nations of the world. China is a communist country that has drawn the ire of multiple human rights groups for their abuses. Additionally, "China has an expanding body of strategic interests in the greater Middle East region. This is manifested in its security relationships with Saudi Arabia, Iran, and Pakistan, which entail WMD and ballistic missile cooperation."[188]

Saudi Arabia is tired of the stipulations and 'baggage' that the Americans bring. Militarily, the Saudis wanted the US out of their country after Desert Shield/Storm. Diplomatically, the US-Saudi relationship began to waver post 9/11. Now, the economic relationship is beginning to decline with a renewable energy policy, leaving too few carrots and one tired stick for the US to use in the region. Saudi Arabia already has China as their leading oil customer and therefore will be able to withstand any US drop in oil demand. China has arrived on the scene with all of the attributes that the Americans displayed post World War II – a

---

[188] Richard Russell, "China's WMD Foot in the Greater Middle East Door," *Middle East Review of International Affairs,* 9, no. 3 (September 2005): 108 http://www.ciaonet.org/olj/meria/meria_sep05/meria05_rur01.pdf (accessed February 11, 2009).

need for oil, lots of money, military equipment to sell, and no stipulations or caveats to any deals that the Chinese make in the region.

The US is now on another quest to reduce its dependence on foreign oil and as stated earlier, the US expects to achieve a 20% reduction in 10 years, which equates to a small country's GDP being taken off the market. Domestic politics, fueled by a renewable energy policy, will increasingly draw the US out of the Persian Gulf. The renewable energy policy and diminishing market power will begin to degrade the influence the US has in the region, especially as the US is overtaken by China and its energy needs.

As mentioned earlier, a 20% reduction in oil consumption by the US in ten years and a 12% a year demand increase for crude by China means that at some point between 2015 and 2020, China will surpass the US as the world's largest oil consumer, and US oil market power will now be surpassed.

All things being equal, any reduction of oil demand by the US will cause oil prices to maintain stable since China's demand are growing. In this situation, developing and developed countries that are still dependent on oil would enjoy oil prices that remain low and would allow them to continue to grow while the US transitions its economy to a new energy source. This issue becomes particularly problematic if the US adopts policies to force the system to change to new renewable energy systems that may not be as economically viable as oil, thereby increasing the economic burden and reducing overall GDP in the US. Given the present debt and deficit the US currently holds this scenario is something the US can ill afford. Also, the oil-exporting countries that supported policies that were inimical to US interests when the US was the biggest consumer of oil will still be able to supply China and make plenty of money to continue their goals.

Of further concern to the US is the fact that all the oil in the world is currently traded in US dollars. There has been talk in recent years of switching oil trading from the US dollar to some other denomination, such as the Euro, Ruble, or Dinar to name a few. In fact, Iran just opened, after two years of problems, their own oil bourse and began trading their petrochemicals for Iranian Rials and some other forms of international currency, (but no US dollars).[189]

> [The role of the dollar] enabled the United States to be "far less restrained…than all other states by normal fiscal and foreign exchange constraints when it came to funding whatever foreign or strategic policies it decided to implement." As Robert Gilpin notes, quoting Charles de Gaulle, such policies led to a 'hegemony of the dollar" that gave the U.S. "extravagant privileges." In David Calleo's words, the U.S. government had access to a "gold mine of paper" and could therefore collect a subsidy from foreigners in the form of seignorage (the profits that flow to those who mint or print a depreciating currency).[190]

American has enjoyed this position for years and the conversion of the oil market from the dollar to another currency may not occur. However, it is hard to deny that if countries are considering this change now, how much more attractive will they consider it as the US reduces its consumption of oil and China becomes the thirsty giant on the planet? Of further concern on the economic front is how much US debt the Chinese and Saudi Arabia will be holding. For reference, as of December 2008, China held $727.4 billion of US debt and oil exporting countries (includes Saudi Arabia) held $186.2 billion dollars of Treasury securities for a total of $913.6 billion dollars.[191] It is important to note here that this includes Treasuries only, not investments by Sovereign Wealth Funds into the security and assets market. This has

---

[189] "Iranian Oil Bourse Starts Trading, Sans Dollar Contracts," Seeking Alpha, http://seekingalpha.com/article/65003-iranian-oil-bourse-starts-trading-sans-dollar-contracts (accessed January 21, 2009).

[190] Niall Ferguson. (2003). Hegemony or Empire. "Review of Two Hegemonies: Britain 1846-1914 and the United States 1941-2001," edited by Patrick Karl O'Brien and Armand Clesse, *Foreign Affairs, 82*(5), 154-161. Retrieved March 11, 2009, from ABI/INFORM Global database. (Document ID: 389028911).

[191] "Major Foreign Holders of Treasury Securities," U.S. Department of Treasury, http://www.treas.gov/tic/mfh.txt (accessed March 11, 2009).

increasingly led to numerous concerns about the 'dumping' of the US dollar. "For example, in the past, some Chinese officials reportedly suggested that China could dump (or threaten to dump) a large share of its holdings to prevent the United States from imposing trade sanctions against China over its currency policy."[192]

Diplomatically, the Chinese have cooperated on some issues with the US, but on the more troubling international problems, the Chinese have thwarted US efforts. "China negotiated deals to supply Iran (and also Pakistan) with equipment and technology useful for making nuclear weapons, despite having signed the Nuclear Nonproliferation Treaty."[193] China holds a Security Council vote at the UN and has become a key obstacle to US efforts to put international pressure on Iran over their quest to obtain a nuclear weapon.[194] China is also a key supplier of arms and military equipment to many of the countries in the Middle East, to include Israel.

Further concerns of a China-Saudi bilateral relationship will be the reaction of oil-importing countries around the world that still need oil. Increasingly, out of their own national-interest, they will side with China and Saudi Arabia to ensure they curry favor with them to ensure their supply of oil. This has happened in the past during the 1973 Arab-Oil embargo when the Europeans, who imported 80% of their oil from the Middle East and the Japanese, who imported 90%, began switching from pro-Israeli to pro-Arab policies.[195] If the US gradually

---

[192] Wayne Morrison and Marc Labonte, Congressional Research Service Report RL34314, *China's Holdings of US Securities: Implications for the US Economy,* February 26, 2009.

[193] Barry Rubin, "China's Middle East Strategy," *Middle East Review of International Affairs* 3, no. 1 (March 1999): under "Nuclear," http://meria.idc.ac.il/journal/1999/issue1/jv3n1a4.html (accessed February 23, 2009).

[194] Robin Wright, "Iran's New Alliance With China Could Cost U.S. Leverage," *Washington Post*, November 17, 2004, under "A21," http://www.washingtonpost.com/wp-dyn/articles/A55414-2004Nov16.html (accessed March 11, 2009).

[195] Branislav Slantchev, "National Security Strategy: The Rise and Fall of D´etente, 1971-1980," *University of California, San Diego* (March 2, 2005): 8 http://polisci.ucsd.edu/...bslantch/courses/nss/lectures/19-detente-malaise.pdf (accessed February 11, 2009).

withdraws from the oil market and their influence in the region decreases, those countries still needing oil will lean toward policies favored by China or Saudi Arabia.

"America's unipolar moment, it seems, was brief, and the world now appears to be moving rapidly toward multipolarity or what one analyst has termed the 'post-American' era."
-Michael Schiffer

CONCLUSION:

"Classic international relations theory holds that during periods of "power transition," when shifting power relations between nations create new patterns of power distribution, there are dangers that a misalignment of communications, expectations, perceptions, and legitimacy among major powers can lead to breakdowns and the potential for conflict throughout the international order."[196]

The strategic and operational risks of reducing US consumption of oil are real and should be of concern of strategists and military planners alike. It is a popular statement today to proclaim that reducing American dependence on foreign oil will benefit the national security interests of the US. Reducing consumption of oil is not a panacea to US foreign policy in the Middle East and in fact, leaves policy makers and Presidents with fewer options. There may be long term gains from a renewable energy policy that reduces our consumption of oil, but in the short term, there will be significant risks as we reverse engineer over 60+ years of foreign and military policy that has been concerned with the access and free flow of oil. As stated earlier, oil represents an almost $2 trillion dollar a year business and to have the US not have a stake in this market will certainly cause concern from some countries and will bring about opportunities for other nation states to flex themselves onto the world stage. The US can still spread its influence around the world but that influence will be greatly diminished without a valuable negotiating tool as oil. The US exerts serious influence in the world oil market, and therefore, world oil geopolitics by being the world's largest consumer of oil. As the US weans itself from oil, it will

---

[196] Michael Schiffer, "The U.S. and rising powers," Foreign Policy Association, http://www.fpa.org/topics4707/topics_show.htm?doc_id=697438 (accessed January 15, 2009).

find itself increasingly isolated from other superseding powers in their quest to influence, negotiate, and ensure access to energy markets that will be vital to those nations' national security. Other emerging powers' quests for oil access will lead to bilateral and potentially multilateral arrangements based on the need to produce and/or consume oil. As US oil demand decreases, the ability to negotiate with the "oil card" will diminish as producers will gladly look to growing consumers so that producing states can maintain their economies. Concern over oil is a matter of vital national security to almost every developed or developing nation state in the world. As such, the concern for oil leads to multiple bilateral and multilateral agreements among other nations and it is through these agreements that national concerns to be addressed.

If that logic isn't convincing enough, let history be the guide. Just prior and during World War II, the United States' main concern for involvement in Saudi Arabia was oil and strategic access to the region. The relationship started as an arrangement of oil for security and trade subsequently led to military training and arms sales and the building of numerous agreements, both formal and informal. The connection continued to build with military security agreements to collusion for the fight against communism in Egypt and Afghanistan. With this bilateral relationship came a moderation of policies and concerns, by both sides, for the entire Middle East. It would have been much more difficult for the US to have any influence in the region without this relationship. With a renewable energy policy and a few years' time, China will replace the US in the region. The question is if China will act in the United States' best interests. The answer is that it will probably depend.

Daniel W. Drezner writes in an article in the *National Interest,* "In short, a world that doesn't need oil may also be a world that doesn't need the United States."[197] The real fear is that

---

[197] Daniel W. Drezner, *Oil Dependence As Virtue,* National Interest online, October 30, 2008 (accessed January 8, 2009).

a US that doesn't need oil, will find itself in a world that doesn't need the US. The National Intelligence Council hypothesized of "A World Without the West" in their fourth installment of *Global Trends 2025: A Transformed World.* In this world, new powers supplant the US as it withdraws because it feels overburdened in Central Asia and Afghanistan.[198] In this account, "Russia and China enter a marriage of convenience; other countries – India and Iran – rally around them. The lack of any stable bloc – whether in the West of the non-Western world – adds to growing instability and disorder, potentially threatening globalization."[199]

Throughout history there has been an ebb and flow of nation states. The question of whether we are truly at the end of American hegemony or merely in a period of rising nation states to a multi-polar world is hard to tell. What is clear is that a shift to renewable energy policies by the United States will only hasten its exit from world dominance. Contrary to the many pundits who believe that reducing our dependence on oil is the right course to follow, it is more important to be a part of the game than to stand on the sidelines or sit in the stands. Those options leave the US with no influence, merely a bystander watching the events. On the field one may get roughed up or muddy, but at least one is part of the game and can influence the outcome. For example, it was discussed earlier how the US and Saudi Arabia worked a plan that eventually led to the downfall of the Shah of Iran and the rise of a radical theocracy. Like Libya in 2004, one wonders what might happen if the US made the same sort of efforts with Iran. Could the US have gone to Iran with an effort to buy large volumes of Iranian crude in exchange for concessions on their nuclear program? It is an intriguing question to ask, but one whose possibility continually diminishes as the US begins to implement renewable energy policies.

---

[198] *Global Trends 2025,* 4.

[199] Ibid, 4.

Bibliography:

Atkinson, Rick. *An Army at Dawn, The War in North Africa, 1942-1943*. New York: Henry Holt and Company, LLC, 2002.

"ABC News/Planet Green/Stanford University poll, July 23-28, 2008." Polling Report. http://www.pollingreport.com/energy.htm (accessed January 15, 2009).

"Annual Energy Report." Energy Information Administration. http://www.eia.doe.gov/aer/txt/ptb1105.html (accessed November 15, 2008).

"Annual Energy Review." Energy Information Administration. http://www.eia.doe.gov/emeu/aer/pdf/pages/sec5.pdf, (accessed December 3, 2008).

Bacevich, Andrew. "The Real World War IV." *Wilson Quarterly* 29, no. 1 (Winter 2005). http://www.proquest.com/ (accessed February 17, 2009).

"Background Notes, Ecuador." U.S. Department of State. http://www.state.gov/r/pa/ei/bgn/35761.htm (accessed March 5, 2009).

Bader, Jeffrey A. and Richard C. Bush, III. "Contending with the Rise of China, Three Decades of Progress," in *Opportunity 08, Independent Ideas for America's Next President,* Michael E. O'Hanlon, editor, (Washington D.C.: Brookings, 2007).

Blanchard, Christopher M. Congressional Research Service report RL33533, *Saudi Arabia: Background and U.S. Relations,* (2008).

Bronson, Rachel. *Thicker Than Oil: America's Uneasy Partnership with Saudi Arabia*. New York: Oxford University Press, 2006.

Bronson, Rachel. "What Saudi Arabia Wants - Good Neighbors." Saudi-US Relations Information Service. http://www.saudi-us-relations.org/articles/2007/ioi/070417p-bronson-neighbors.html (accessed February 25, 2009).

Cassidy, John. "The Coming Oil Crash." Conde Nast Portfolio. http://www.portfolio.com/views/columns/economics/2007/12/17/Why-Oil-Prices-Will-Drop (accessed January 10, 2009).

"China, Ecuador: Beijing's Latin American Opportunity." Stratfor. http://www.stratfor.com/analysis/china_ecuador_beijings_latin_american_opportunity (accessed March 3, 2009).

"China's Thirst for Oil." *International Crisis Group* (9 June 2008). http://www.ciaonet.org/wps/icg/0001342/0001342.pdf (accessed February 23, 2009).

"CleanTech Venture Investments by US Firms Break Record in 2007." PR Newswire. http://www.prnewswire.com/cgi-bin/stories.pl?ACCT=104&STORY=/www/story/11-28-2007/0004712795&EDATE (accessed January 15, 2009).

Cook, Steven A. (2008). Disentangling Alliances: America in the Middle East. *The American Interest, 4*(1), 78-86. Retrieved March 11, 2009, from ProQuest Social Science Journals database. (Document ID: 1544727731).

Cooper, Andrew Scott. "Showdown at Doha: The Secret Oil Deal That Helped Sink the Shah of Iran." *The Middle East Journal* 62, no. 4 (October 1, 2008): 567-591. http://www.proquest.com/ (accessed March 4, 2009).

Cordesman, Anthony. "Saudi Arabia Enters the Twenty-First Century: The Political, Foreign Policy, Economic, and Energy Dimensions." *Praeger Security International* (2003). http://psi.praeger.com/doc.aspx?newindex=1&q=Saudi+Arabia+security+concerns&c=&d=/books/dps/200094ab/200094ab-p200094ab9970041001.xml&i=1#txmlhit (accessed March 11, 2009).

"Country Brief: Libya." Energy Information Administration. http://www.eia.doe.gov/cabs/Libya/Oil.html (accessed January 23, 2009).

"Crude Oil Price History." New York Stock Exchange. http://www.nyse.tv/crude-oil-price-history.htm (accessed November 15, 2008).

Downs, Erica. "China's Quest for Energy Security." *Rand Corporation* (2000). http://www.rand.org/pubs/monograph_reports/MR1244/ (accessed February 23, 2009).

Drezner, Daniel W., *Oil Dependence As Virtue,* National Interest online, October 30, 2008 (accessed January 8, 2009).

Duffield, John. *Over a Barrel, The Costs of U.S. Foreign Oil Dependence*. Stanford: Stanford University Press, 2008.

Dumbaugh, Kerry. Congressional Research Service Report RL 34588, *China's Foreign Policy: What Does It Mean for U.S. Global Interests?*, (2008).

"Energy and the Environment." the White House, President Barack Obama, http://www.whitehouse.gov/agenda/energy_and_environment/ (accessed January 18, 2009).

"Energy Timeline from 1971 to 1980." Department of Energy. http://www.energy.gov/about/timeline1971-1980.htm (accessed January 3, 2009).

"Fact Sheet: Twenty in Ten: Strengthening Energy Security and Addressing Climate Change." The White House, President George W. Bush, http://georgewbush-whitehouse.archives.gov/news/releases/2007/05/20070514-2.html (accessed February 3, 2009).

Ferguson, Niall. (2003). Hegemony or Empire. "Review of Two Hegemonies: Britain 1846-1914 and the United States 1941-2001," edited by Patrick Karl O'Brien and Armand Clesse, *Foreign Affairs, 82*(5), 154-161. Retrieved March 11, 2009, from ABI/INFORM Global database. (Document ID: 389028911).

"From peril to progress (Update 1: Full Remarks)," the White House, President Barack Obama, http://www.whitehouse.gov/blog_post/Fromperiltoprogress/ (accessed February 3, 2009).

Geller, Howard. "Strategies for Reducing Oil Imports: Expanding Oil Production vs. Increasing Vehicle Efficiency." American Council for an Energy Efficient Economy. http://www.aceee.org/pubs/e011.pdf (accessed January 11, 2009).

Gray, Colin. *Another Blood Century*. London: Phoenix, 2004.

Henderson, Simon. "Chinese-Saudi Cooperation: Oil but also Missiles," The Washington Institute for Near East Policy, http://www.ciaonet.org/pbei/winep/policy_2006/2006_1095/2006_1095.html (accessed February 12, 2009).

Heilbroner, Robert, and Aaron Singer. *The Economic Transformation of America: 1600 to the Present,*. San Diego: Harcourt Brace Jovanovich, 1984.

Henriksen, Thomas. "Is Leaving the Middle East a Viable Option?" *Joint Special Operations University* (08-1-2008).

"History of Energy in the United States: 1635-2000," Energy Information Administration, http://www.eia.doe.gov/emeu/aer/eh/frame.html (accessed February 23, 2009).

"How Dependent Are We on Foreign Oil?"." Energy Information Administration. http://tonto.eia.doe.gov/energy_in_brief/foreign_oil_dependence.cfm (accessed November 15, 2008).

"Iranian Oil Bourse Starts Trading, Sans Dollar Contracts." Seeking Alpha. http://seekingalpha.com/article/65003-iranian-oil-bourse-starts-trading-sans-dollar-contracts (accessed January 21, 2009).

Jiang, Wenran. "China's Quest for Energy Security." *The Jamestown Foundation* 4, no. 20 (October 14, 2004). http://www.ciaonet.org/pbei-2/jfcb/jfcb_v4_20/jfcb_v4_20.pdf (accessed February 12, 2009).

Joffe, George. "Why Gaddafi gave up WMD." BBC News. http://news.bbc.co.uk/2/hi/africa/3338713.stm (accessed February 23, 2009).

Kho, Jennifer. "Greentech VC Hits $2.6B in U.S." Greentech Media. http://www.greentechmedia.com/articles/greentech-vc-hits-26b-in-us-332.html (accessed January 15, 2009).

Kretzman, Steve. "Oil, Security, War: The Geopolitics of U.S. Energy Planning." *The Multi-National Monitor* 24, no. 1 (Jan/Feb 2003).

LaMonica, Martin. "Obama signs stimulus plan, touts clean energy." cnet news. http://news.cnet.com/8301-11128_3-10165605-54.html (accessed March 2, 2009).

Lippman, Thomas. *Inside the Mirage: America's Fragile Partnership with Saudi Arabia.* Boulder: Westview Press, 2004.

Lippman, Thomas. "The Day FDR Met Saudi Arabia's King Ibn Saud." *The Link* 38, no. 2 (April-May 2005). http://www.ameu.org/uploads/vol38_issue2_2005.pdf (accessed March 4, 2009).

Miller, Keith. "How Important was Oil in World War II?" History News Network. http://hnn.us/articles/339.html, (accessed November 15, 2008).

Morrison, Wayne and Marc Labonte. Congressional Research Service Report RL34314, *China's Holdings of US Securities: Implications for the US Economy,* (2009).

National Security Council. Directive 26/3, *Subject: Demolition and Abandonment of Oil Facilities and Fields in the Middle East*, June 29, 1950.

National Security Council. Directive 54, *Responding to Iraqi Aggression in the Gulf,* January 15, 1991.

National Security Council. Directive 63, *Subject: Persian Gulf Security Framework*, January 15th, 1981.

"New Energy for America." Barack Obama and Joe Biden. http://my.barackobama.com/page/content/newenergy (accessed January 18, 2009).

"Part 5: The Obama Administration and the Middle East." Stratfor, Global Intelligence. http://www.stratfor.com/analysis/20090218_part_4_obama_administration_and_middle_east (accessed February 23, 2009).

Pollack, Kenneth. "Securing the Gulf." *Foreign Affairs* 82, no. 4 (Jul/Aug 2003).

Ramazani, R.K. "Security in the Persian Gulf." *Foreign Affairs* 57, no. 4 (Spring79 1979): 821-835. *Military & Government Collection*, EBSCOhost (accessed March 4, 2009).

"Rank Order – GDP (Purchasing Power Parity)." 2006 CIA World Fact Book. http://www.umsl.edu/services/govdocs/wofact2007/rankorder/2001rank.html, (accessed March 3, 2009).

"Rank Order - GDP (purchasing power parity)." Central Intelligence Agency, The World Fact Book. https://www.cia.gov/library/publications/the-world-factbook/rankorder/2001rank.html (accessed March 2, 2009).

Razavi, Hosain, and Firouz Vakil. *The Political Environment of Economic Planning in Iran, 1971-1983*. Boulder: Westview Press, 1984. Quoted in Andrew Scott Cooper

Rubin, Barry. "China's Middle East Strategy." *Middle East Review of International Affairs* 3, no. 1 (March 1999). http://meria.idc.ac.il/journal/1999/issue1/jv3n1a4.html (accessed February 23, 2009).

Russell, Richard. "China's WMD Foot in the Greater Middle East Door." *Middle East Review of International Affairs,* 9, no. 3 (September 2005). http://www.ciaonet.org/olj/meria/meria_sep05/meria05_rur01.pdf (accessed February 11, 2009).

Rutledge, Ian. *Addicted to Oil: America's Relentless Drive for Energy Security*. London: I.B. Tauris, 2005.

Safran, Nadav. *Saudi Arabia, The Ceaseless Quest for Security*. Ithaca: Cornell University Press, 1985.

Sandalow, David. *Freedom from Oil*. New York: McGraw Hill, 2008.
"Saudi Arabia: a chronology of the country's history and key events in the US-Saudi relationship." PBS Frontline. http://www.pbs.org/wgbh/pages/frontline/shows/saudi/etc/cron.html, (accessed February 13, 2009).

"Saudi Arabia." Central Intelligence Agency, The World Fact Book. https://www.cia.gov/library/publications/the-world-factbook/geos/sa.html (accessed March 2, 2009).

Schiffer, Michael. "The U.S. and rising powers." Foreign Policy Association. http://www.fpa.org/topics4707/topics_show.htm?doc_id=697438 (accessed January 15, 2009).

Sick, Gary. *The Middle East and the United States: A Historical and Political Reassessment*. Edited by David Lesch. Boulder: Westview Press, 2003

Sissine, Fred. Congressional Research Service report RL33831, *Energy Efficiency and Renewable Energy in the 110th Congress*, (2007).

Slantchev, Branislav. "National Security Strategy: The Rise and Fall of D´etente, 1971-1980." *University of California, San Diego* (March 2, 2005). http://polisci.ucsd.edu/...bslantch/courses/nss/lectures/19-detente-malaise.pdf (accessed February 11, 2009).

Steingart, Gabor. *The War for Wealth*. New York: McGraw Hill, 2008.

Stine, Deborah D. Congressional Research Service Report RL34645, *The Manhattan Project, the Apollo Program, and Federal Energy Technology R&D Programs: A Comparative Analysis,* (2008).

"Saudi Arabia: Feeling the Iranian Pinch in Iraq." STRATFOR. http://www.stratfor.com/saudi_arabia_feeling_iranian_pinch_iraq (accessed February 11, 2009).

Tarbell, Ida. *The History of The Standard Oil Company.* New York: McClure, Phillips, and Co, 1904.

Telhami, Shilbey, and Fiona Hill. "Does Saudi Arabia Still Matter?" *Foreign Affaris* 81 (Nov/Dec 2002).

Toosi, Nahal. "Clinton Debuts $1B Renewable-Energy Fund." CBS News. http://www.cbsnews.com/stories/2006/09/22/ap/politics/mainD8KA10K00.shtml (accessed January 15, 2009).

The Economist. Special Report: Waking up and catching up – Green America. January 27, 2007.

"The Story of Oil in Pennsylvania," Paleontological Research Institution, www.priweb.org/ed/pgws/history/pennsylvania/pennssylvania.html, (accessed October 20, 2008).

"There's a Lot of Life in a Barrel of Oil," American Petroleum Institute, http://www.api.org/classroom/tools/upload/oilfacts_rgb.pdf (accessed November 12, 2008).

"Toyota Worldwide Hybrid Sales Top 1 Million Units." Toyota. http://www.toyota.co.jp/en/news/07/0607.html (accessed January 6, 2009.).

"United States Energy Profile." Energy Information Administration. http://tonto.eia.doe.gov/country/country_time_series.cfm?fips=US (accessed March 3, 2009).

U.S. Department of Defense, Annual Report to Congress, *Military Power of the Peoples Republic of China 2007.*

U.S. Department of Energy, *On the Road to Energy Security, Implementing a Comprehensive Energy Strategy: A Status Report,* Secretary Samuel W. Bodman.

U.S. Department of State, *Joint Communiqué on the First Session of the U.S.—Saudi Arabian Joint Commission on Economic Cooperation, constituting an agreement on economic cooperation.* Done at Washington on 27 February 1975. Registered by the United States of America on 7 May 1976.

"U.S. Imports by Country of Origin." Energy Information Administration. http://tonto.eia.doe.gov/dnav/pet/pet_move_impcus_a2_nus_ep00_im0_mbbl_m.htm (accessed January 15, 2009).

U.S. Joint Forces Command, *The Joint Operating Environment 2008, Challenges and Implications for the Future Joint Forces,* November 2008.

U.S. National Intelligence Council, *Global Trends 2025: A Transformed World,* (Washington DC: US Government Printing Office, 2008).

U.S. President, Speech, "State of the Union Address," January 23, 1980, http://www.jimmycarterlibrary.org/documents/speeches/su80jec.phtml, accessed December 15, 2008.

"Major Foreign Holders of Treasury Securities." U.S. Department of Treasury. http://www.treas.gov/tic/mfh.txt (accessed March 11, 2009).

Vella, Matt. "Diesels Come Clean." *Business Week*, March 26, 2007. http://www.businessweek.com/autos/content/mar2007/bw20070326_220157.htm?chan=autos_autos+index+page (accessed January 6, 2009).

"Venezuela." Central Intelligence Agency, The World Fact Book. https://www.cia.gov/library/publications/the-world-factbook/print/ve.html (accessed March 2, 2009).

Yergin, Daniel. *The Prize, The Epic Quest for Oil, Money, and Power*. New York: Touchstone, 1991.

Yetiv, Steven, and Chunlong Lu. "China, Global Energy, and the Middle East." *The Middle East Journal* 61, no. 2 (Spring 2007).

Yetiv, Steve and Lowell Feld. "*America's Oil Market Power,"* World Policy Institute, 2008.

Zinga, Susan. "What Does the Energy Policy Act of 2005 Mean for Energy Efficiency?" *Southface Journal* (Fall 2005). http://www.southface.org/web/resources&services/publications/journal/sfjv305/sfjv305-energy_policyact_2005.htm (accessed January 18, 2009).

Zhu, Winnie and Wang Ying. "Sinopec, Aramco May Agree on Oil Supply, Refinery (Update1)." Bloomberg.com. http://www.bloomberg.com/apps/news?pid=20601207&sid=a0QhDUVADLJg&refer=energy (accessed March 9, 2009).